PERIODIC TABLE

Janet Bingham

Every attempt has been made to clear copyright. Should there be any inadvertent omission, please apply to the publisher for rectification. **BOOK** Alamy: 10–11c (Sergey Uryadnikov), 10cr (Andreas Prott), 14–15c (Sean Pavone), 16cl (Dimitar Todorov), 17tr (sciencephotos), 18–19c (Westend61 GmbH), 20bl (funkyfood London – Paul Williams), 22 cr (The Granger Collection), 26bl (Ian Canham), 32bl (Len Wilcox), 34br (Science Photo Library), 38–39c (GFC Collection), 40c (Arterra Picture Library), 43cr (Scenics & Science), 46cl (ONEWORLD PICTURE), 52–53c (John Henshall), 53tl (Scenics & Science), 58br (Science History Images), 60cl (World History Archive), 60br (Grant Heilman Photography), 66bl (Ian Dagnall), 68cl (Alon Meir), 70c (Science History Images), 76–77c (Indiapicture), 77tr (Ron Giling), 78–79c (Marcelo Mayo), 78c (Gibson Green), 82bl (Laboratory), 84–85c (Science Photo Library), 86–87c (Science Photo Library), 86bl (Kim Christensen), 90tr (Paul Doyle), 94cr (B. David Cathell), 96–97c (GRANGER – Historical Picture Archive)/ Shutterstock, 101tr (NG Images), 102cr (agrofruti), 104–105c (Tetra Images, LLC), 112cl (Gado Images), 113bl (stockeurope), 118–119c (Gado Images), 118br (Sueddeutsche Zeitung Photo), 119br (Science Photo Library), 120–121c (Nick Harrison), 121br (Science History Images), 122–123c (dpa picture alliance), 124cr (Associated Press). **Lorraine Inglis:** 56br. **NASA:** 4–5c (NASA/CXC/MIT/L.Lopez et al; Infrared: Palomar; Radio: NSF/NRAO/VLA). **Royal Society of Chemistry (Murray Robertson):** 29 tr, 35t, 44bl, 64br, 81 tr, 83br, 91tr, 93tr, 103tr, 104bl, 106bl, 108bl, 111tr, 115bc, 121tr. **Science Photo Library:** 8br (ALEXANDRE DOTTA / SCIENCE SOURCE), 28–29c (JULIEN ORDAN), 47tr (THIERRY BERROD, MONA LISA PRODUCTION), 50cr (MARTYN F. CHILLMAID), 86c (CONEYL JAY). **Shutterstock:** 4cr (Rost9), 4br (YEVHENIIA BUNHA), 5tl (Aleksey Sagitov), 5cr (saran insawat), 5cr (White Space Illustrations), 5bl (sirtravelalot), 6–7 c (2DAssets), 8–9 c (WBMUL), 8cl (Rostislav Ageev), 10cl (BlueRingMedia), 11tr (BlueRingMedia), 12–13 c (Bedrin), 12cl (chuteye), 12br (Sansanorth), 13tr (Jaswe), 14cl (zizou7), 14cr (Dream01), 15tl (Sansanorth), 16–17 c (ShutterStockStudio), 16cl (John Erickson), 18cl (mpohodzhay), 18br (Danijela Maksimovic), 20–21 c (Virag Nobile), 20cr (Chris J Bradshaw), 21t (Dionisvera), 22–23 c (Pavel Sapozhnikov), 23tr (GGW), 24–25 c (Sarunyu L), 24bl (trgrowth), 24br (trgrowth), 26–27c (Pike–28), 26cr (Sansanorth), 27cr (Designua), 28c (OSweetNature), 28bl (Michael Dechev), 30–31c (Paopano), 30c (PeopleImages.com – Yuri A), 30bl (PIYA_BUNMALERD), 31br (TorriPhoto), 32–33c (Georgios Tsichlis), 32c (VDB Photos/Shuttterstock), 33tr (sanek59), 34–35c (Fredy Thuerig), 34cl (Adisak Riwkratok), 36–37c (Oleg Kovtun Hydrobio), 36c (Mariia Korneeva), 36bl (petrroudny43), 37cr (Basilico Studio Stock), 38cl (Pixel-Shot), 38br (Sebastian Janicki), 39tr (Alexander Piragis), 40–41c (White bear studio), 40bl (Aleksandr Kondratov), 41br (MEE KO DONG), 42–43c (Phonlamai Photo), 42cl (Vladimir Zhoga), 42br (pryzmat), 44–45c (YAKOBCHUK VIACHESLAV), 44c (Joe Belanger), 45br (Anneka), 46–47c (Yellowj), 46tr (FotoHelin), 46br (Peter Hermes Furian), 48–49c (Dmitry Kalinovsky), 48c (Thong19), 48bl (Yuriy Golub), 49tr (Tawansak), 50–51c (YARUNIV Studio), 50bl (My Ocean Production), 51tr (rweisswald), 52c (Andrey_Popov), 52bl (Marco Frino Fotografo), 54–55c (Gerald Robert Fischer), 54tr (Jacek Chabraszewski), 54cr (Evannovostro), 55tr (Jacek Rogoz), 56–57c (SHI1116), 56c (Prostock–studio), 57cr (DIVA. photo), 58–59c (Nordroden), 58cl (TetiBond), 59t (Africa Studio), 60–61 (frank_peters), 61tr (FoxGrafy), 62c (lunamarina), 62cl (Clash and Clash), 62br (Peyker), 63c (Bogdan Vija), 64–65c (asharkyu), 64c (e_rik), 65cr (Salayenko), 66–67c (Petro Perutskyi), 66c (Emily Marie Wilson), 67tr (Photooongraphy), 68–69c (azur13), 68br (filippo giuliani), 69tr (Roman Zaiets), 70–71c (kongsky), 70br (RHJPhtotos), 71cr (heidi birch photos), 72–73c (StockLite), 72cr (Parilov), 74–75c (Photology1971), 74tr (grafvision), 74cr (dekazigzag), 75c (Anna Chavdar), 76c (Vandy Apeldo), 76bl (Droneyes), 78bl (EGT–1), 79cr (Michael Cola), 80–81c (Mikhail Markovskiy), 80bl (STEKLO), 80br (LanKS), 82–83c (W. de Vries), 82tr (simonekesh), 84cl (hacohob), 84cb (aslysun), 85cr (New Africa), 87cr (Chokniti–Studio), 88–89c (Dmytro Sheremeta), 89tr (Nick Greaves), 88bl (Salim October), 89br (RHJPhtotos), 90br (Svyatoslav Balan), 90br (Roman Voloshyn), 92–93c (Andrey_Popov), 92tr (J Paulson), 92cl (Roman Chazov), 94–95c (Proxima Studio), 96c (Monkey Business Images), 98–99c (New Africa), 98c (AgriTech), 99tr (ssuaphotos), 100–101c (Orhan Cam), 100br (New Africa), 102–103 (Serhiy Stakhnyk), 103bl (Shan_shan), 104c (Martin Pelanek), 105tr (wasy_cat), 106tr (MarcelClemens), 107tr (Boonchuay1970), 107bl (TKalinowski), 108–109c (Anelo), 108cr (YEVHENIIA BUNHA), 109tr (AnilD), 110–111c (Ondrej Prosicky), 110tr (Bjoern Wylezich), 110cr (Parilov), 112–113c (hrui), 112br (magnetix), 114–115c (Phonlamai Photo), 114bl (Claudio Caridi), 116–117c (Hafiz Johari), 116cr (Dima Zel), 118c (Paramonov Alexander), 120tr (Prachaya Roekdeethaweesab), 122c (Emir Kaan), 124–125c (zhengzaishuru). **Wikimedia Commons:** 7tr, 9br, 10br, 13br, 14br, 17tr, 19br, 21br, 22bl, 25br, 98bl. **FACT CARDS** (listed by number of element). **Alamy** 3 Phil Degginger / Alamy Stock Photo, 4 Ron Evans / Alamy Stock Photo, 6 horst friedrichs / Alamy Stock Photo, 11 sciencephotos / Alamy Stock Photo, 17 Bob Daemmrich / Alamy Stock Photo, 18 Kim Christensen Alamy Stock Photo, 19 Phil Degginger / Alamy Stock Photo, 38 FotoHelin / Alamy Stock Photo, 48 SBS Eclectic Images / Alamy Stock Photo, 77 Rosanne Tackaberry / Alamy Stock Photo, 90 John Cancalosi / Alamy Stock Photo. **Science Photo Library** 55 SCIENCE PHOTO LIBRARY. **Shutterstock** 1 Scharfsinn/Shutterstock, 2 Pra Chid/Shutterstock, 5 Bjoern Wylezich/Shutterstock, 7 Athapet Piruksa/shutterstock, 8 Nina B/Shutterstock, 9 Albert Russ/Shutterstock, 10 Martyn Jandula/Shutterstock, 12 usk75/Shutterstock, 13 arturnichiporenko/Shutterstock, 14 RHJPhtotos/Shutterstock, 15 StockVisual/Shutterstock, 16 Jira Po/Shutterstock, 20 Bjoern Wylezich/Shutterstock, 21 Minakryn Ruslan/Shutterstock, 22 AB–7272/Shutterstock, 23 Bjoern Wylezich/ Shutterstock, 24 Suponev Vladimir/Shutterstock, 25 RHJPhtotos/Shutterstock, 26 Jiri Balek/Shutterstock, 27 liliya Vantsura/Shutterstock, 28 Steve Mann/Shutterstock, 29 Flegere/shutterstock, 30 Bjoern Wylezich/Shutterstock, 31 Dima Zel/Shutterstock, 32 Joaquin Corbalan P/Shutterstock, 33 ju_see/Shutterstock, 34 LuYago/Shutterstock, 35 Qutaibah thawabi/Shutterstock, 36 LuYago/Shutterstock, 42 RHJPhtotos/Shutterstock, 46 RHJPhtotos/Shutterstock, 50 changphoto/Shutterstock, 51 Albert Russ/Shutterstoc , 56 Diego Sugoniaev/Shutterstock, 57 Bjoern Wylezich/ Shutterstock, 76 LuYago/Shutterstock, 79 Vitaly Korovin/Shutterstock, 80 Ventin/Shutterstock, 92 RHJPhtotos/ Shutterstock, 118 saran insawat/Shutterstock. **BOX** All Shutterstock: Top Shutterstock isak55. Bottom Vladi333. Left side Julia-art. Right side Weerachai Khamfu **BOOK COVER** All Shutterstock: Front cover isak55. Back cover Creative Travel Projects. Spine Julia-art.

This edition published in 2024 by Arcturus Publishing Limited
26/27 Bickels Yard, 151–153 Bermondsey Street,
London SE1 3HA

Copyright © Arcturus Holdings Limited

All rights reserved. No part of this publication may be reproduced, stored in a retrieval system, or transmitted, in any form or by any means, electronic, mechanical, photocopying, recording, or otherwise, without prior written permission in accordance with the provisions of the Copyright Act 1956 (as amended). Any person or persons who do any unauthorized act in relation to this publication may be liable to criminal prosecution and civil claims for damages.

CH011547US
Supplier 13, Date 0924, PI00008102

Printed in China

Author: Janet Bingham
Consultant: Anne Rooney
Designer: Lorraine Inglis
Picture research: Lorraine Inglis
and Paul Futcher
Editor: Becca Clunes
Design manager: Rosie Bellwood-Moyler
Managing editor: Joe Harris

CONTENTS

Introduction ... 4

Chapter 1
Organizing the Elements ... 6

The Periodic Table ... 6
Elements and Chemicals ... 8
Atoms and Matter ... 10
Atomic Structure ... 12
Atomic Bonds ... 14
Periodic Table Structure ... 16
Metals and Nonmetals ... 18
The Earliest Chemistry ... 20
The First Periodic Table ... 22
Reading the Periodic Table ... 24

Chapter 2: Hydrogen to Argon
Periods 1, 2, and 3 ... 26

Hydrogen ... 26
Helium ... 28
Lithium, Beryllium ... 30
Boron ... 32
Carbon ... 34
Nitrogen, Oxygen ... 36
Fluorine, Neon ... 38
Sodium, Magnesium ... 40
Aluminum, Silicon ... 42
Phosphorus ... 44
Sulfur ... 46
Chlorine, Argon ... 48

Chapter 3: Potassium to Krypton
Period 4 ... 50

Potassium ... 50
Calcium ... 52
Scandium, Titanium, Vanadium ... 54
Chromium, Manganese ... 56
Iron ... 58
Cobalt, Nickel ... 60
Copper, Zinc ... 62
Gallium, Germanium ... 64
Arsenic, Selenium ... 66
Bromine, Krypton ... 68

Chapter 4: Rubidium to Xenon
Period 5 ... 70

Rubidium, Strontium ... 70
Yttrium to Technetium ... 72
Ruthenium, Rhodium, Palladium ... 74
Silver ... 76
Cadmium, Indium ... 78
Tin ... 80
Antimony, Tellurium, Iodine ... 82
Xenon ... 84

Chapter 5: Cesium to Radon
Period 6 ... 86

Cesium, Barium ... 86
Lanthanum, Cerium ... 88
Praseodymium to Samarium ... 90
Europium, Gadolinium, Terbium ... 92
Dysprosium to Lutetium ... 94
Hafnium to Osmium ... 96
Iridium, Platinum ... 98
Gold ... 100
Mercury ... 102
Thallium, Lead ... 104
Bismuth, Polonium, Astatine, Radon ... 106

Chapter 6: Francium to Oganesson
Period 7 ... 108

Francium, Radium ... 108
Actinium, Thorium, Protactinium ... 110
Uranium ... 112
Neptunium, Plutonium, Americium ... 114
Curium to Mendelevium ... 116
Nobelium, Lawrencium ... 118
Rutherfordium, Dubnium, Seaborgium ... 120
Bohrium to Copernicium ... 122
Nihonium to Oganesson ... 124

GLOSSARY ... 126

INDEX ... 128

Introduction

Chemistry is the scientific study of "stuff," or matter—from water and rocks to human-made substances. All matter is made from elements. The elements are the building blocks of all other substances, and the Periodic Table is the key to understanding them.

> We are all made of elements that were forged inside stars and scattered into space in supernova explosions.

Elements in Order

The Periodic Table ranks the elements by atomic number, in order of size. This book examines the elements one by one—where they're found, how they look and behave, which ones we need, and which ones are deadly poisons.

Atomic Structure

An atom is the smallest possible piece of an element. We know which element an atom belongs to by the number of even tinier, subatomic particles inside it.

A million atoms could line up across the cut surface of a human hair.

Groups and Periods

The Periodic Table's neat Groups and Periods reveal "periodicity"—elements in the same vertical column, or Group, have similar properties and seem to belong together.

We can predict that any Group 2 element will be a silvery metal that's more reactive than the element above it in the Group.

Some of the most spectacular chemical reactions are seen in fireworks displays.

Reactions

Atoms react. They make bonds, like us holding hands. This joins the elements into compounds that are completely different chemicals.

Odd Similarities

The two most chemically reactive elements are flourine and cesium. One is a metal and one's a gas—the Periodic Table helps explain why they are both so reactive.

The Periodic Table is still used today. It helps scientists to develop new materials that are cheaper, more efficient, and better for the enironment.

Chemistry Through the Ages

Throughout history, scientists have studied matter. The Periodic Table, drawn up by Dmitri Mendeleev in 1869, organized the knowledge of the time in a new way—and encouraged scientists to find unknown elements and to synthesize (make) new atoms.

Chapter 1: Organizing the Elements

The Periodic Table

Everything in our Universe—including us—is made of chemicals. Out of thousands of chemicals, just 118 are elements—the simplest chemicals that are building blocks for all the rest.

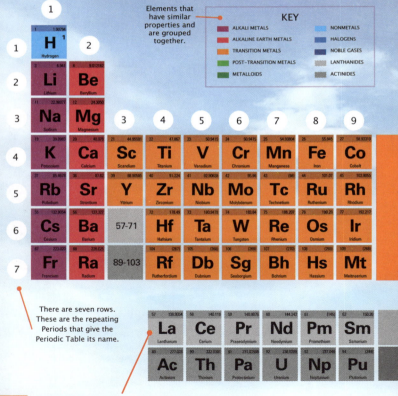

Elements that have similar properties and are grouped together.

KEY
- ALKALI METALS
- ALKALINE EARTH METALS
- TRANSITION METALS
- POST-TRANSITION METALS
- METALLOIDS
- NONMETALS
- HALOGENS
- NOBLE GASES
- LANTHANIDES
- ACTINIDES

There are seven rows. These are the repeating Periods that give the Periodic Table its name.

The lanthanides are very similar elements in squares 57 to 71.

Size Order

The Periodic Table sorts the elements by the size of their atoms (see pages 12–13). The rows of squares are read from left to right, from the lightest, hydrogen, to the heavyweight, oganesson. We can learn a lot about an element from its position in the rows and columns.

Shorthand Symbols

Each element has a symbol. Some are easy short forms—like H for hydrogen. Others are harder to remember—like Na for sodium. An element's atomic number shows its place on the Table. Its atomic mass is its relative weight (its weight compared to other atoms).

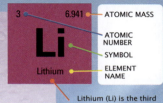

ATOMIC MASS
ATOMIC NUMBER
SYMBOL
ELEMENT NAME

Lithium (Li) is the third element on the Table. Its atomic mass shows one atom weighs nearly seven times as much as a hydrogen atom.

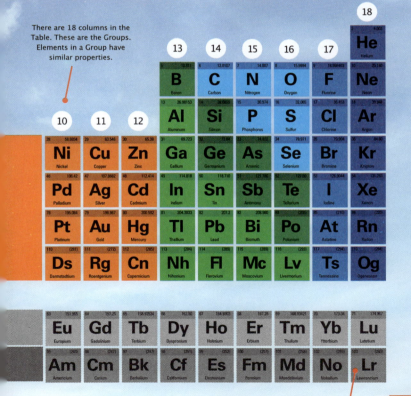

There are 18 columns in the Table. These are the Groups. Elements in a Group have similar properties.

The actinides are in squares 89 to 103. Lanthanides and actinides are shown separately to make the Table less crowded.

Elements and Chemicals

Elements are the simplest chemicals—they are made of just one kind of atom. But atoms don't keep things simple—they combine using chemical bonds. The atoms of fewer than 100 elements can combine to make thousands of chemicals.

Compounds and Mixtures

The atoms of sodium (Na) and chlorine (Cl) combine to create a compound called sodium chloride. Its chemical formula—NaCl—shows that one sodium atom bonds with one chlorine atom. We know NaCl as table salt. One oxygen (O) atom and two hydrogen (H) atoms bond to make water (H_2O). Atoms can also mix together without bonding. Air is a mixture of gases.

Air is 78 percent nitrogen, 21 percent oxygen, and 1 percent other gases and water vapor. Divers and astronauts sometimes breathe pure oxygen.

An uncooked sponge cake is a mixture of ingredients (impure). The ingredients react chemically during cooking—you can't unbake a cake.

Pure and Impure

Substances that contain only one thing are called "pure." It could be one element, like gold, or one compound, like water. We can't take anything out of a pure substance without changing it chemically. An impure substance is a mixture of elements or compounds. They can be separated—like peas from pasta—without a chemical reaction.

A mixture of iron filings and sand can be easily separated because the iron is magnetic and the sand isn't.

DID YOU KNOW? You contain around 1 octillion atoms—that's 1 followed by 27 zeros. Your atoms were made inside stars—or even just after the Big Bang.

NOTABLE MOMENTS: Humphry Davy
1807–1808

Humphry Davy was a British chemist born in 1778. He invented electrochemistry—the study of electricity in chemical reactions. Davy used the newly invented battery to break apart chemical compounds by electrolysis. In 1807 and 1808, he isolated potassium, sodium, calcium, strontium barium, and magnesium in this way.

> The gas in a helium balloon is just helium atoms—it's a pure element. Helium is lighter than air, so it floats.

> Pure sugar contains nothing except sugar. Sugar is a compound of carbon, hydrogen, and oxygen.

> A carbonated or fizzy drink is a mixture of flavored water and carbon dioxide (CO_2) gas. The CO_2 escapes as the bubbles rise to the top.

Atoms and Matter

All matter—everything around us—is made up of tiny particles. They are atoms, or groups of atoms, called molecules. Imagining these particles as tiny balls can help explain why solids, liquids, and gases behave differently. This is the particle theory of matter.

States of Matter

Solid, liquid, and gas are the states of matter. A solid doesn't change shape. Liquids and gases flow and change shape to fit their containers—they are fluids. Solids and liquids have a definite volume and density, but gases expand because their atoms or molecules float apart.

Japanese macaques bathe in hot springs where heated underground water flows up to the surface.

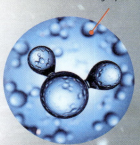

A water molecule contains one oxygen and two hydrogen atoms. Water molecules move around, but the three atoms are tightly bonded.

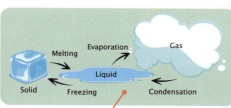

The tightly held particles in solids can only jiggle (vibrate). As they gain energy, the bonds loosen and the solid melts. As the bonds loosen more, the liquid becomes gas.

NOTABLE MOMENTS:
John Dalton
1803

The English scientist John Dalton was born in 1766. Chemists at the time knew that matter was made of tiny particles (atoms), but they thought all atoms were alike. Dalton understood that each element has its own kind of atom. His atomic theory from 1803 is based on atoms of different elements having different size and mass.

10

Changing States

Things change state—liquid water freezes to ice, and ice melts in the sun. Changes of state are physical, reversible changes. They depend on temperature, or when particles gain energy and move farther apart as they heat up. That makes gases less dense than liquids, and liquids usually less dense than solids.

Chemicals change states at particular temperatures. Chemists use the different melting and boiling points to identify chemicals.

As water freezes, the molecules are held together by strong bonds. The ice melts when the temperature rises.

The steam is water vapor. Some water molecules break free of the liquid and escape into the air. This is evaporation.

If a liquid is heated to its boiling point, all the molecules gain enough energy to escape, making gas.

DID YOU KNOW? There is a fourth state of matter—plasma, or ionized gas. We see plasma in lightning, in the Northern Lights, and in decorative plasma lamps.

Atomic Structure

> The atom's nucleus is massive—heavy for its size—because it contains protons and neutrons.

Atoms are made of smaller subatomic particles—protons, neutrons, and electrons. Different elements have different numbers of subatomic particles. The Periodic Table arranges the elements by size, as their atoms get more particles.

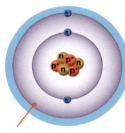

Lithium has atomic number 3. Its nucleus has three protons. This isotope has three neutrons. Three electrons are arranged in two surrounding energy shells.

Protons and Electrons

Protons are in the nucleus (center) of an atom. The number of protons defines an element and its place on the Table. This is its atomic number. Protons have mass and a positive charge, so the nucleus is positive. Electrons have almost no mass and a negative charge. They exist in energy shells (also called electron shells) outside the nucleus. An atom has equal numbers of protons and electrons—so the whole atom has no charge.

Neutrons

Neutrons are in the nucleus. They have mass but no charge. The number of protons plus neutrons in an atom is its mass number. An element can have atoms with different numbers of neutrons—these are isotopes. Atomic mass is an average of the mass of an element's isotopes, so it can have a decimal point.

Oxygen atoms have eight protons and eight electrons. The most common isotope, oxygen-16, has eight neutrons. Other isotopes have nine or ten.

Oxygen-16
8 Electrons
8 Protons
8 Neutrons

Mass number
= 8 + 8 = 16

Oxygen-17
8 Electrons
8 Protons
9 Neutrons

Mass number
= 8 + 9 = 17

Oxygen-18
8 Electrons
8 Protons
10 Neutrons

Mass number
= 8 + 10 = 18

The first energy shell, nearest the nucleus, can contain up to two electrons. The second shell can contain eight.

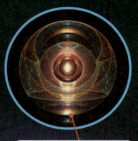

Imagine an atom's electrons whizzing about in concentric clouds—shells—around the nucleus. The shells are like force fields where electrons are held by electromagnetic force.

Bigger atoms have more shells. Each shell fills up with electrons before another shell is added farther out from the nucleus.

Outside the nucleus, the atom is mostly empty. The electrons are held by the equal and opposite charge of the protons.

NOTABLE MOMENTS:
Ernest Rutherford
1911

Ernest Rutherford was a New Zealand physicist born in 1871. In 1911, he fired positively charged alpha particles at very thin gold leaf. Most passed through, showing that the atom is mostly empty space. Some bounced back, showing positive charge in the center of the atom. Rutherford had discovered the nucleus and its positively charged particle—the proton.

DID YOU KNOW? If an atom was as big as a US football stadium, the nucleus would be like a pea in the middle with electrons whizzing around the stadium's edge.

13

Atomic Bonds

Each energy shell in an atom can hold a given number of electrons. When it's full, it is stable and unreactive, and another shell can be added. Atoms with spaces in their shells bond with other atoms by attracting or donating electrons to achieve full shells. The bonds are electrical forces of attraction.

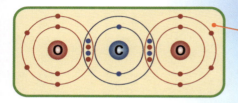

A carbon dioxide molecule is formed with covalent bonds. One carbon atom and two oxygen atoms share electrons. They all end up with an outer shell filled with eight electrons.

Covalent and Ionic Bonding

In a chemical reaction, the bonds made by electrons combine the atoms into a structure called a molecule. A covalent bond is when atoms bond by sharing electrons. An ionic bond is when one atom loses electrons to another atom. An atom that has lost or gained an electron is an ion. It has a positive or negative charge, and it's attracted to ions with the opposite charge.

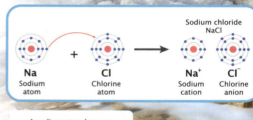

A sodium atom loses an electron to a chlorine atom to make a positively charged sodium ion (Na+) and a negative chlorine ion (Cl-).

NOTABLE MOMENTS: Joseph John Thomson 1897

The electron was discovered in 1897 by English physicist, J.J. Thomson. His experiments with cathode rays—seen when electricity flows through gases—showed streams of particles with much less mass than atoms. He concluded that all atoms contain these particles—we now call them electrons.

Diamond — Tetrahedral
Graphite — Trigonal planar
Fullerene — Spherical

In diamond, carbon atoms make four bonds. In graphite, they make three bonds, forming sheets weakly held together. Fullerene is another carbon allotrope.

Allotropes

Identical atoms may bond to make molecules of a pure element. Some bond in different patterns to make surprisingly different allotropes (forms) of the element. Diamond is the hardest natural substance on Earth, and graphite (pencil lead) is very soft. Yet diamond and graphite are both allotropes of carbon.

Salt crystals form naturally in the Dead Sea. They are sodium chloride—a compound of the metal sodium and the toxic gas chlorine.

Table salt is sodium chloride. Salt crystals have straight edges because sodium and chlorine atoms link up in a neat pattern.

Sodium metal conducts electricity because electrons can flow through it. In sodium chloride, electrons are tightly held in ionic bonds, so salt doesn't conduct electricity.

Sodium chloride is a giant ionic lattice. It is a cubic crystal of alternating sodium ions and chlorine ions.

DID YOU KNOW? Scientists believe high atmospheric pressures on Saturn turn carbon atoms into 907 tonnes (1,000 tons) of diamond rain every year.

15

Periodic Table Structure

The Periodic Table lists the atoms by atomic number. Each atom has one more proton than the atom before. It also has one more electron, because atoms have as many electrons as protons.

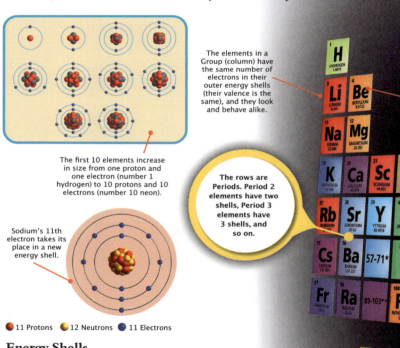

The elements in a Group (column) have the same number of electrons in their outer energy shells (their valence is the same), and they look and behave alike.

The first 10 elements increase in size from one proton and one electron (number 1 hydrogen) to 10 protons and 10 electrons (number 10 neon).

The rows are Periods. Period 2 elements have two shells, Period 3 elements have 3 shells, and so on.

Sodium's 11th electron takes its place in a new energy shell.

● 11 Protons ● 12 Neutrons ● 11 Electrons

Energy Shells

The energy shells in an atom can hold a certain number of electrons. The first shell is full when it has two electrons, and the second shell is full with eight electrons. As each shell fills up, another shell appears outside it. The Periodic Table begins a new row with each new shell.

DID YOU KNOW? Small atoms are stable with equal numbers of neutrons and protons. Larger atoms need more neutrons. Lead (82 protons) is stable with 126 neutrons.

Valence

Valence is bonding power. It depends on the number of electrons that can make a bond. Group 18 atoms have valence of 0 (unreactive) because their outer shell is full, so no electrons can bond. Group 1 atoms have valence of 1—their outer shell has one electron, which is easily given away. Group 17 atoms also have valence of 1—they attract one electron to fill their outer shell.

> Group 1, the alkali metals, react spectacularly with water and often explode.

> Period 2 elements have an inner (first) shell containing two electrons, and a second shell containing a number of electrons from 1 (lithium) up to 8 (neon).

> The 18 Groups have names. Group 2 is the alkaline earth metals. Group 17 is the halogens.

| 5 B BORON 10.811 | 6 C CARBON 12.011 | 7 N NITROGEN 14.007 |
| 13 Al ALUMINUM 26.98 | 14 Si SILICON 28.085 | 15 P PHOSPHORUS 30.974 |

NOTABLE MOMENTS:
William Ramsay
1894

In 1894, William Ramsay, with Lord Rayleigh, discovered the first noble gas by isolating it from air. The new gas was "astonishingly indifferent"—it would not react with any other element. They named it argon (meaning "inert"). Ramsay found more, similar elements, and added Group 18—the noble gases—to the Periodic Table.

Metals and Nonmetals

Most elements are metals. They are on the left and middle of the Periodic Table. The nonmetals are on the right. Around the zigzag line between them are the metalloids, or semi-metals—elements that sometimes act like metals.

> Metals are usually hard, strong, and shiny, with high melting and boiling points. They conduct heat and electricity. They can be easily shaped and clang when hit.

Chemical Reactions

Metals and nonmetals react differently. Metals make ionic bonds with nonmetals by donating electrons to form ions, while nonmetals react with other nonmetals by sharing electrons in covalent bonds. Metals react with acids, while nonmetals usually don't. Metals react with oxygen to form oxides that make alkaline solutions with water, while nonmetal oxides are acidic.

Silicon is a metalloid. It's brittle like a nonmetal, but it sometimes conducts electricity like a metal. It's used to make silicon chips in electronics.

Transition Metals

Elements in the central block (Groups 3–12) of the Table are transition metals. They have special powers. When they bond, they use electrons from different levels (orbitals) inside their energy shells. This makes different oxidation states—ions with different charges. For example, copper gives up one electron to form Cu^+ ion and gives up two electrons to form Cu^{2+} ion.

Chromium(II) Cr^{2+}
Chromium(III) Cr^{3+}
Monochromate CrO_4^{2-}
Dichromate $Cr_2O_7^{2-}$

DID YOU KNOW? Hydrogen is a nonmetal. Like other nonmetals, it can become metallic under very high pressures—such as in the center of Jupiter.

All our electronic devices are built around semiconductors made from metalloids like silicon.

Nonmetals are usually poor conductors of heat and electricity, with low melting and boiling points. Plastics are nonmetals.

Carbon is an important nonmetal. Living things are made of organic chemicals—molecules with a backbone of carbon atoms with hydrogen, oxygen, and other elements attached.

NOTABLE MOMENTS: Irène Joliot-Curie 1935

Irène Joliot-Curie and her husband, Frederic Joliot, jointly won the Nobel Prize for Chemistry in 1935 for turning one element into another. They did it by firing helium nuclei at a thin aluminum sheet. The helium nuclei altered the number of subatomic particles in some of the aluminum nuclei, changing them into a radioactive isotope of phosphorus.

The Earliest Chemistry

Through the ages, people have found resources, from herbs to metals, to make what they needed. Curiosity about materials has gradually turned into modern science—the systematic study of the world.

> In the Middle Ages, important manuscripts were decorated (illuminated) using pigments from natural sources.

Philosophers

By 500 BCE, early philosophers (deep thinkers) were wondering what matter was made of. Ancient Greek philosophers like Aristotle believed that earth, air, fire, and water were the four elements (simple substances) that made up everything. Aristotle's ideas led to the study of substances and the early science of alchemy.

Early hunter-gatherers discovered that plants were not just food—some could be used as medicines or poisons—or to make dyes.

Prehistoric people knew about metals. They worked pure metals like gold and copper and improved them by mixing them into alloys.

Herbalists and Alchemists

While medieval herbalists and healers were making recipes for medicines and cosmetics, alchemists were looking for the mythical philosopher's stone. They believed it would cure illness and turn ordinary metals into gold. They began developing experimental methods and laboratory equipment, and they discovered real elements and compounds. The work of herbalists and alchemists led to modern chemistry.

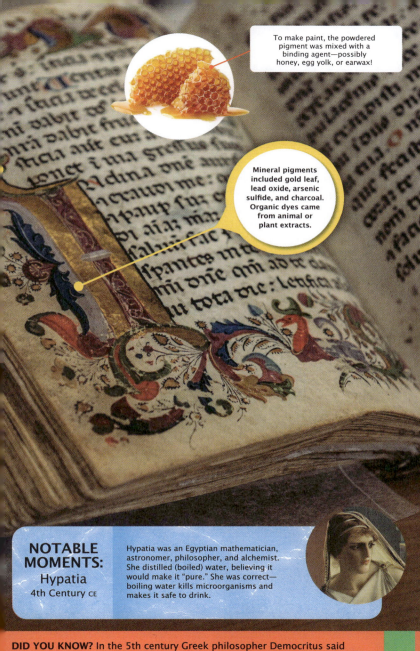

To make paint, the powdered pigment was mixed with a binding agent—possibly honey, egg yolk, or earwax!

Mineral pigments included gold leaf, lead oxide, arsenic sulfide, and charcoal. Organic dyes came from animal or plant extracts.

NOTABLE MOMENTS: Hypatia
4th Century CE

Hypatia was an Egyptian mathematician, astronomer, philosopher, and alchemist. She distilled (boiled) water, believing it would make it "pure." She was correct—boiling water kills microorganisms and makes it safe to drink.

DID YOU KNOW? In the 5th century Greek philosopher Democritus said matter was made of tiny particles he called "atomos." The idea didn't catch on for centuries!

The First Periodic Table

By the end of the 18th century, around 40 elements were known. Antoine Lavoisier first tried classifying them in 1789. As more elements were discovered, scientists began to look for better ways to arrange them.

Dmitri Mendeleev's Periodic System was the first version to be accepted by the scientific community.

Dmitri Mendeleev

Nineteenth-century scientists arranged the known elements by relative atomic mass. In 1869, Russian chemist Mendeleev—the Father of the Periodic Table—noticed patterns, like very reactive nonmetals were followed by very reactive light metals. Mendeleev also noticed some elements were missing. He left gaps and predicted their properties—and they were discovered later.

Antoine Lavoisier grouped the elements into gases, nonmetals, metals, and earths.

John Newlands

In 1865, just before Mendeleev published his Periodic Table, British chemist Newlands presented his Law of Octaves. It correctly showed that, in a list of known elements, every eighth one had similar properties. He did not leave spaces for undiscovered elements, and his paper was rejected.

DID YOU KNOW? Pre-1774, scientists believed things that burned gave off "phlogiston" gas—and that they stopped burning when the air was full.

NOTABLE MOMENTS: Bunsen & Kirchhoff 1859

In 1859, Robert Bunsen and Gustav Kirchhoff invented the spectroscope to separate the colors of light given off by burning chemicals. Their analysis revealed two new elements—cesium in mineral water and rubidium in the mineral lepidolite. The flame tests were done with a Bunsen burner—which Bunsen also invented.

The noble gases were unknown until the 1890s, after Mendeleev designed his Table.

Mendeleev thought carefully about the table. Iodine should come before tellurium, because it has less mass. That seemed the wrong way around, so Mendeleev reversed them. The discovery of isotopes later showed he was right.

A monument in Saint Petersburg, Russia, commemorates Mendeleev's work.

Mendeleev first put similar elements in horizontal rows, but then placed them in vertical columns instead—heralding the Groups and Periods of our Periodic Table.

23

Reading the Periodic Table

The Periodic Table shows the periodicity of the elements—similar properties occur at regular intervals in the list. So we can guess how an element will look and behave from its atomic number and its position on the Table.

> An element's atomic number tells us the electronic structure of the atom. Oxygen is number 8—so it has eight protons and eight electrons.

Periodicity

The Table begins a new horizontal row (Period) each time a new energy shell is added in the list of atoms. So elements in a vertical Group all have the same number of electrons in their outer shell. That gives them similar physical and chemical properties, or periodicity.

Group 18—the noble gases—have an increasing number of energy shells, but they all have a full outer shell. They are unreactive.

Group 1 elements all have one electron in the outer shell. The last electron is easily given away in reactions, especially by the larger atoms.

Group 17

Elements in Group 17 (halogens) have seven electrons in the outer shell. We can predict they'll react easily with other elements, because they only need to attract one more electron to fill the shell. The halogens' reactivity decreases as we read down the Group. This is because the nucleus attracts other electrons, but that force gets weaker as the atom and shell structure get bigger.

NOTABLE MOMENTS: Lise Meitner 1938

Lise Meitner was a physicist born in Austria in 1878. She studied radioactivity for 30 years. Her research with Otto Hahn and Fritz Strassmann, firing neutrons at uranium, led to the discovery of nuclear fission (splitting the nucleus) in 1938. The artificial element meitnerium (number 109) was named in her honor in 1982.

DID YOU KNOW? The elements after uranium (number 92) are too big to exist naturally on Earth. Scientists create them in laboratories, but often they decay in milliseconds.

25

Chapter 2: Periods 1, 2, and 3: Hydrogen to Argon

Hydrogen

Group 1; Period 1; one proton; one electron in one energy shell. This is the smallest, simplest, and most important atom—hydrogen.

> Our Universe has areas of hydrogen and dust where new stars form. In the Eagle Nebula, 6,500 light-years away, the hydrogen and dust form great pillars.

Essential for Life

Hydrogen is the lightest gas. It's not an alkali metal even though it's in Group 1. But, like alkali metals, it has one very reactive electron. It readily reacts to form compounds, and it's inside all the molecules of life. With oxygen it forms water, and unique hydrogen bonds between the molecules give water special life-supporting properties.

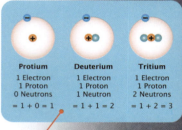

Protium
1 Electron
1 Proton
0 Neutrons
= 1 + 0 = 1

Deuterium
1 Electron
1 Proton
1 Neutron
= 1 + 1 = 2

Tritium
1 Electron
1 Proton
2 Neutrons
= 1 + 2 = 3

Most hydrogen is protium. There are two other isotopes—deuterium has one neutron, and tritium has two neutrons.

Hydrogen and oxygen react inside fuel cells to make electricity to run an electric car. The only byproduct is water.

Applications

Hydrogen is used in the fertilizer, pharmaceutical, food, and plastics industries, and in electronics and glass-making. It has an important role in new, cleaner fuels, but production of hydrogen itself requires electricity, risking environmental harm. Hydrogen's explosive reaction with oxygen is also a safety concern.

DID YOU KNOW? An estimated 9 out of 10 atoms in the Universe are hydrogen atoms.

Helium

With two protons and two neutrons, helium is the second smallest atom. Like hydrogen, it's lighter than air, but it behaves very differently—because helium's energy shell is complete, with two electrons. It's the second and last element in Period 1.

> CERN's Large Hadron Collider (LHC) is a particle accelerator. Scientists bash high-speed atomic particles together, looking for new particles.

Made in Space and Earth

Helium was produced just after the Big Bang. It's also made in stars, and produced on Earth when underground uranium emits alpha-particles. Alpha-particles are helium nuclei. Their positive charge grabs free electrons and they become helium atoms. They have two protons and two neutrons.

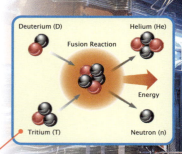

Helium is made in stars by the fusion of the nuclei of deuterium and tritium (hydrogen isotopes).

Most Unreactive

Helium is the most unreactive element of all, so it makes a good inert, protective atmosphere for optical fibers and semiconductors for electronic devices. It has the lowest boiling point of the elements, so it can cool materials to very low temperatures, making it an important coolant in refrigeration and the space industry. Helium-neon lasers are in supermarket barcode scanners.

An 80% helium and 20% oxygen mixture is easier for sick babies to breathe than pure oxygen.

DID YOU KNOW? Helium cools the LHC's magnets to –271 °C (–456 °F), which is even colder than the –270 °C (–454 °F) temperature of space.

Helium comes from the Latin word for "sun." The element was first detected in the Sun's corona in 1868, 28 years before being found on Earth.

Powerful electromagnets that steer the particle beam through the 27-km (17-mile) ring tunnel are cooled with liquid helium.

At such low temperatures, the magnets' coils lose electrical resistance and become more efficient superconductors.

2 4.003
He
Helium

Atomic number: 2
Melting point: unknown
Boiling point: −269 °C (−452 °F)
Earth crust: trace amount
Year of discovery: 1895
Group: 18
Category: noble gas

29

Lithium

Lithium has three electrons. Two fill up the first energy shell, and the third begins a second shell, so lithium starts Period 2. It's the lightest metal, and it's reactive. It fizzes in water, and when it's cut, the silvery metal quickly reacts with air and darkens.

Rechargeable Batteries

Batteries are lithium's most important use. It makes small, light batteries for heart pacemakers and rechargeable batteries for laptops and vehicles. Adding it to aluminum makes an alloy that is strong and light. Aluminum-lithium alloys are used in bikes, planes, and high-speed trains.

Lithium demand could soar as electric vehicles increase, but this risks environmental harm from mining.

To reduce the need for lithium mines, scientists are working on zinc batteries. Chitin from crab shells could be used to protect the zinc from corrosion.

Atomic number: 3
Melting point: 181 °C (357 °F)
Boiling point: 1,342 °C (2,448 °F)
Earth crust: 16 ppm
Year of discovery: 1817
Group: 1
Category: alkali metal

DID YOU KNOW? Lithium chloride aborbs water from the air. It is used in air conditioning systems and factories.

Beryllium

Beryllium is a silvery-white, soft, low-density metal. It's the first of the alkaline earth metals (Group 2). They are named for their oxides—alkaline earths—which make alkaline solutions in water.

Transparent to X-rays

Beryllium is rare, expensive, and toxic, but it has remarkable properties. A substance can be X-rayed inside a beryllium container because beryllium lets X-rays pass through without interfering with the procedure. Alloys of beryllium with copper and nickel have higher conductivity and good elasticity—useful for making springs and non-sparking tools.

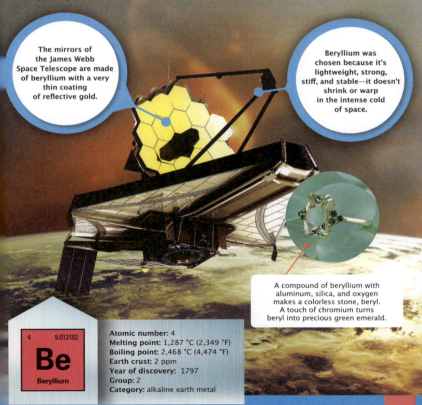

The mirrors of the James Webb Space Telescope are made of beryllium with a very thin coating of reflective gold.

Beryllium was chosen because it's lightweight, strong, stiff, and stable—it doesn't shrink or warp in the intense cold of space.

A compound of beryllium with aluminum, silica, and oxygen makes a colorless stone, beryl. A touch of chromium turns beryl into precious green emerald.

4   9.012182
Be
Beryllium

Atomic number: 4
Melting point: 1,287 °C (2,349 °F)
Boiling point: 2,468 °C (4,474 °F)
Earth crust: 2 ppm
Year of discovery: 1797
Group: 2
Category: alkaline earth metal

Boron

Boron is the first metalloid on the Periodic Table. It's a boring-looking, brown, amorphous (non-crystalline) powder, but it also has a hard, black, crystalline form.

> Boron is essential for plant growth. In the 1930s, ancient olive groves in Greece and Spain had poor fruit crop yields.

Borates

Most boron is found as sodium borate (borax) and calcium borate. Borax is very important. Together with boric acid and boric oxide, it's used in eye drops, antiseptics, laundry powder, and tile glazes. Borax has also been used in bleaches and as a food preservative. For centuries, the only known deposits were at Yamdrok Lake, China, but Turkey and the USA are now the major producers.

Boric oxide is used to make heat-resistant borosilicate glass (Pyrex), used for baking dishes and insulation.

The world's largest borax mine, is in the Mojave Desert, USA. The town of Boron was built around it.

Surprising, not Boring

Boron nitride has carbon-like allotropes. One is almost as hard as diamond and used in abrasives; the other is soft like graphite and used in cosmetics. Boron trihydride was considered impossible in 1945, until a student worked out its structure. Since then, boron clusters—human-made molecules—have been developed for use in medicine.

DID YOU KNOW? The original Persil laundry powder was a mixture of (and named after) sodium perborate and sodium silicate.

Boron gives a green flame. It's used in flares and is safer than barium in fireworks.

The cell walls of plants can't develop properly without boron.

The olive crops improved after the trees were given fertilizer with the boron compound disodium octaborate tetrahydrate.

Trace amounts of boron keep our bones healthy. Boron in fruit and vegetables gives us around 2 mg of boron every day.

5 10.811
B
Boron

Atomic number: 5
Melting point: 2,077 °C (3,771 °F)
Boiling point: 4,000 °C (7,232 °F)
Earth crust: 11 ppm
Year of discovery: 1808
Group: 13
Category: metalloid

33

Carbon

Uniquely, carbon atoms bond in strong chains, like a backbone, with hydrogen atoms attached. These molecules are hydrocarbons. Fossil fuels are hydrocarbons that we use as raw materials to make petrochemicals, chemicals, and plastics.

Plants capture carbon dioxide (CO_2), using it to build glucose by photosynthesis. Animals eat the plants, and carbon passes through the food chain.

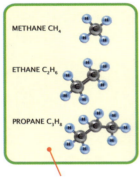

METHANE CH_4

ETHANE C_2H_6

PROPANE C_3H_8

In the hydrocarbon series starting with methane, each molecule has one carbon and two hydrogen atoms more than the one before, building up very long chains.

Basis of Life

We are made of carbon-based, organic chemicals. Molecules of carbon and hydrogen with other atoms, like oxygen, make the huge range of molecules in living things. For example, glucose ($C_6H_{12}O_6$) is a simple sugar. Plants and animals use glucose for metabolism—the chemical reactions of life—to grow and build healthy bodies.

Different Forms

Carbon allotropes are forms with different properties, from super-hard diamond to slippery graphite—the "lead" in pencils. In industry, carbon fiber is used to make strong, lightweight objects, and activated carbon (with high surface area) to filter and purify. Nanotechnologists are developing new molecular structures, such as conductive nanotubes just one atom thick, for electronics.

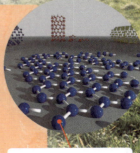

Graphene is an atom-thick sheet of graphite with a hexagonal pattern of atoms.

DID YOU KNOW? The largest protein in your body is titin. A titin molecule contains at least 169,719 carbon atoms.

This artistic representation of carbon acknowledges its nickname, King of the Elements. The name refers to the unique bonding abilities of its atoms, making different forms.

Greenhouse gases trap the infrared radiation that naturally keeps Earth warm enough for life. Upsetting the balance with too much CO_2 causes climate change.

Carbon's boiling point is the same as its melting point because liquid carbon doesn't exist at atmospheric pressures. When carbon is heated to its boiling point, it sublimes, or turns directly into a gas.

Fossil fuels—coal, oil, and gas—are ancient stores of carbon. Burning them has raised CO_2 in Earth's atmosphere from 280 ppm 150 years ago, to 425 ppm in 2024.

Animals and plants release CO_2 in respiration. Carbon returns to the environment through breathing, waste, and decaying plants and animals.

6	12.0107
C	
Carbon	

Atomic number: 6
Melting point: 3,825 °C (6,917 °F)
Boiling point: 3,825 °C (6,917 °F)
Earth crust: 200 ppm
Year of discovery: prehistory
Group: 14
Category: nonmetal

Nitrogen

Earth's atmosphere is 78 percent nitrogen. It's essential to plants and animals, and important to the chemicals industry—but it's not easy to use because it exists in air as very unreactive diatomic molecules. The strong pair-bonds must be broken before the atoms can make compounds.

Nitrogen Fixing

Paired nitrogen atoms are separated naturally by nitrogen-fixing bacteria in the roots of plants like clover, and in industry by the Haber process. Nitrogen is used in fertilizers, nitric acid, dyes, and explosives. Because nitrogen gas is so stable, it makes an unreactive atmosphere for electronics, research, and keeping food fresh. Liquid nitrogen is used as a refrigerant.

Chefs use liquid nitrogen to make ice cream or add "smoke" effects to party food.

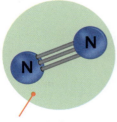

A diatomic molecule contains two identical atoms. Nitrogen atoms pair up with very strong triple bonds.

Atomic number: 7
Melting point: −210 °C (−346 °F)
Boiling point: −196 °C (−320 °F)
Earth crust: 19 ppm
Year of discovery: 1772
Group: 15
Category: nonmetal

DID YOU KNOW? An adult's pee in a year contains 4 kg (9 lb) of nitrogen—enough to grow wheat to make a small loaf of bread.

Oxygen

Oxygen makes up 21 percent of Earth's atmosphere and 46 percent of the crust. It is the third most abundant element in the Universe, after hydrogen and helium. And it is the most abundant element in Earth's crust, mostly as silicon dioxide.

Aerobic Life

Most living things are aerobic. They need oxygen to live. We breathe in oxygen all the time. In nature, it's recycled through the oxygen cycle. In industry, it's used in welding, in waste treatment, and in chemicals and plastics production. Oxygen is reactive and forms compounds (oxides) easily.

Green plants and algae power the oxygen cycle by photosynthesis. They use the Sun's energy, CO_2, and water to make glucose and a waste product—oxygen.

Blood carries oxygen from the lungs around the body, where it's used in cell respiration. Glucose and oxygen are turned into CO_2, water, and energy for our cells.

Microorganisms called cyanobacteria can be found in freshwater and the oceans. Around 3 billion years ago, they photosynthesizing and this raised oxygen levels enough for animals to evolve.

O — Oxygen
8 — 15.9994

Atomic number: 8
Melting point: −219°C (−362 °F)
Boiling point: −183°C (−297 °F)
Earth crust: 461,000 ppm
Year of discovery: 1774
Group: 16
Category: nonmetal

Fluorine

Fluorine is the first halogen in Group 17. It's a dangerously reactive, pale-green gas. It only needs one electron, and it's tiny, so the nucleus attracts electrons greedily. It is probably the second-most reactive element in the Periodic Table, after cesium.

Most Reactive Nonmetal

Among the nonmetals, fluorine is definitely the most reactive. Its compounds are fluorides. Tiny amounts of fluoride ion (F-) are essential to animals. Fluorine is used in welding, frosting glass, and in plastics.

Fluoride, which is related to flourine, is needed for strong teeth and bones. It's added to toothpaste, and sometimes to drinking water, to help prevent tooth decay.

Fluorine is found in the minerals fluorite and cryolite. The semi-precious stone Blue John is a rare fluorite gem.

9 18.998403
F
Fluorine

Atomic number: 9
Melting point: −220 °C (−363 °F)
Boiling point: −188 °C (−307 °F)
Earth crust: 553 ppm
Year of discovery: 1886
Group: 17
Category: halogen

DID YOU KNOW? Fluorine is used to make nonstick saucepans, plumber's tape, and waterproof clothing

Neon

Neon ends Period 2. Its outer energy shell is full, with eight electrons. Unlike its hyper-reactive neighbor fluorine, neon doesn't make compounds. Like the other noble gases in Group 18, it's unreactive.

Small amounts of neon are found in volcanic gases.

Pure neon makes a red light so intense, it's used for beacons to shine through fog. Mixtures of other gases produce other colors.

Inert and Intense

Neon is a light, colorless, odorless gas. It's formed in stars by nuclear fusion of helium and oxygen, and it's the fifth most common element in the Universe. It's nontoxic and safe because it is inert (unreactive). It's used in advertisements, electronics, diving equipment, lasers, and refrigeration.

Neon signs are glass tubes containing gas at a low pressure. An electric current excites the atoms, and they produce bright neon lights.

10   20.180
Ne
Neon

Atomic number: 10
Melting point: –249 °C (–415 °F)
Boiling point: –246 °C (–411 °F)
Earth crust: trace amount
Year of discovery: 1898
Group: 18
Category: noble gas

Sodium

Period 3 starts with sodium, with three energy shells and one electron in its outer shell. Like all alkali metals (Group 1), sodium is very reactive. The soft silver metal tarnishes in seconds in air and reacts with water.

Salt in our Diet

Sodium is essential to life. We need 2 g a day, to replace salt (sodium chloride) lost in sweat. Sodium ions (Na^+) help transmit nerve signals and regulate water levels. We get salt from table salt, but many people eat too much, which can raise blood pressure.

Butterflies are attracted to salt and minerals in mud.

Baking soda (sodium bicarbonate) breaks down in the heat of the oven and produces carbon dioxide. This is what makes muffins rise.

Atomic number: 11
Melting point: 98 °C (208 °F)
Boiling point: 883 °C (1,621 °F)
Earth crust: 23,600 ppm
Year of discovery: 1807
Group: 1
Category: alkali metal

DID YOU KNOW? The human brain contains 85 billion nerve cells. They transmit messages using sodium–potassium pumps.

Magnesium

The second alkaline earth metal, magnesium, is the lightest metal we can use for most purposes. Lithium and sodium are too reactive, and beryllium is toxic, so we have magnesium in lightweight products like our phones.

Essential for Life

We wouldn't exist without magnesium—it's essential to living things, for photosynthesis in plants, and for enzyme function in people. It's used in animal feed and fertilizers. Several over-the-counter drugs contain magnesium as treatments for indigestion or constipation.

Magnesium metal burns with a bright, white light—used in flares, fireworks, and chemistry lessons and demonstrations.

We produce 850,000 tonnes (937,000 tons) per year of magnesium, mainly extracted from the ocean.

Atomic number: 12
Melting point: 650 °C (1,202 °F)
Boiling point: 1,090 °C (1,994 °F)
Earth crust: 28,104 ppm
Year of discovery: 1755
Group: 2
Category: alkaline earth metal

Plants use magnesium to capture the Sun's energy. A chlorophyll molecule contains 137 atoms, including just one magnesium atom.

Aluminum

The most abundant metal in Earth's crust is aluminum (known as aluminium in countries outside North America). It combines with silicon and oxygen in hundreds of minerals. The silvery metal is light, soft, malleable, and it doesn't corrode. It's probably in your house as kitchen foil or window frames.

On Reflection

A thin coating of aluminum reflects light and heat for use in telescope mirrors, decorations, and toys. Aluminum alloys are strong, lightweight, and malleable, perfect for aircraft and other vehicles. Smelting aluminum takes a lot of energy, but once it's made it can be recycled over and over again.

A reflective disk of aluminum focuses the Sun's energy on the cooking pot in a parabolic solar cooker.

Recycling a drink can uses 5 percent of the energy needed to extract the metal from new. From can collection to recycled product may take just 60 days.

Atomic number: 13
Melting point: 660 °C (1,221 °F)
Boiling point: 2,519 °C (4,566 °F)
Earth crust: 84,149 ppm
Year of discovery: 1825
Group: 13
Category: post-transition metal

DID YOU KNOW? A jumbo jet contains 66,000 kg (73 tons) of aluminum—the weight of around 10 elephants.

Silicon

The second most abundant element in Earth's crust, after oxygen, is silicon. Oxygen and silicon combine in minerals like silicon dioxide, or silica—sand. Silicon is in most rocks, and it's thought to make up 5 percent of Earth's core.

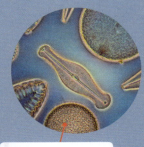

Microscopic algae called diatoms are the only organisms that use silica to construct cell walls. Other organisms use carbon-based compounds.

Basis of Electronics

Silicon doesn't conduct electricity until tiny amounts of doping agents like arsenic are added. Silicon is in all our electronic devices. It makes alloys with aluminum and iron, and it makes silicones—useful, rubbery polymers of silicon and oxygen.

A silicon wafer is a single crystal of silicon. It is hyper-pure, so no imperfections disturb the flow of electrons.

Tiny chips on the wafer are made of silicon doped with impurities, which transforms it into a semiconductor.

Atomic number: 14
Melting point: 1,414 °C (2,577 °F)
Boiling point: 3,265 °C (5,909 °F)
Earth crust: 282,000 ppm
Year of discovery: 1824
Group: 14
Category: metalloid

Phosphorus

Phosphorus has white, red, and black allotropes. The white form is toxic and reactive. It bursts into flames in air and has been used in chemical weapons. But some phosphorus is essential—for us and all life.

Essential for Energy

Phosphorus is in ATP (adenosine triphosphate), the molecule that supplies energy in animal and plant cells. Fertilizer, to replace phosphorus used up from soil, is the largest industrial use. It's also used in animal feed and the steel, electronics, detergent, and chemical industries. The main source is phosphate rock, which could run out.

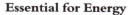

Nontoxic red phosphorus is used in the striking panel on a matchbox.

"Phosphorus" means bringer of light. Four phosphorus atoms bond to make a pyramid-shaped white phosphorus molecule.

Phosphorus is in our bones, cell membranes, DNA molecules (for making proteins), as well as ATP. An adult contains about 750 g (26 oz).

15   30.974
P
Phosphorus

Atomic number: 15
Melting point: 44 °C (111 °F)
Boiling point: 281 °C (537 °F)
Earth crust: 567 ppm
Year of discovery: 1669
Group: 15
Category: nonmetal

Our bodies make and break down ATP molecules all the time. An adult uses up—and rebuilds—their own weight in ATP every day.

Pee for Phosphorus

Many nutrients, like phosphorus and nitrogen, are flushed down the toilet. They, like nutrients from fertilizers and detergents, can pollute rivers. Recycling our flushed-away nutrients into fertilizers would be more sustainable than digging up all the phosphate rock on Earth.

We get phosphorus from foods. Excess phosphorus passes out in our urine (pee) and feces (poop).

DID YOU KNOW? An ordinary African vine grows carnivorous leaves and starts catching insects if it doesn't get enough phosphorus from the soil.

Sulfur

Sulfur is used in rubber, fungicides, and gunpowder, and it is turned into sulfuric acid—a hugely important chemical with many uses, especially in fertilizers. Pure sulfur doesn't smell, but some compounds stink!

Hydrogen sulfide makes rotten eggs stink—and float.

Living Things and Acid Rain

Sulfur is in amino acids, proteins, and enzymes in all living things. Sulfur from living remains in fossil fuels—coal, oil, and gas. Burning unpurified fossil fuels releases sulfur dioxide, causing acid rain and environmental damage. Sulfur is produced a byproduct of fossil-fuel purification.

Pure liquid sulfur on the Ijen volcano, Indonesia, cools to form yellow crystals.

Allotrope Fun

Sulfur has fascinating forms. Gently heated crystalline sulfur melts into a red liquid, which cools to form yellow, monoclinic (needle-shaped) crystals. They change shape into rhombic (pyramidal) crystals as they cool more. But sulfur heated until it boils and cooled quickly, forms stretchy "plastic sulfur," because the heated molecules break and get tangled.

Sulfur crystal molecules have eight atoms in a crown arrangement.

DID YOU KNOW? Sulfur used as a "pest-averting" fumigant is recorded as far back as the 9th century BCE, in Homer's poem The Odyssey.

Chlorine

The second halogen, chlorine, is almost as reactive as fluorine. It's a poisonous, greenish gas with a choking smell. It's heavier than air so it stays close to the ground if it's released.

Good and Bad

Chlorine has two sides. The gas is very toxic, but the chloride ion (Cl⁻) is essential to life, regulating cell fluids. We eat it in table salt. In industry, chlorine is used to make hundreds of products, from bleaches to plastics to pharmaceuticals. Its use is strictly controlled in anesthetics and dry-cleaning solvents.

Chlorine is made into safe disinfectants for drinking water and swimming pools.

We get chlorine and sodium from our diet. These elements are found in table salt (sodium chloride).

Atomic number: 17
Melting point: −102 °C (−151 °F)
Boiling point: −34 °C (−29 °F)
Earth crust: 145 ppm
Year of discovery: 1774
Group: 17
Category: halogen

DID YOU KNOW? Chlorine is used to make PVC. This plastic is used in window frames, car interiors, pipes, electrical wiring, and medical supplies.

Argon

Period 3 ends with argon. Like the other noble gases in Group 18, it's an unreactive, colorless, odorless gas. It is the third most abundant gas, making up nearly 1 percent of the atmosphere.

In electric arc welding, an argon flow of 20 liters (5 gallons) per minute shields the hot aluminum so it doesn't oxidize in air.

Protective Atmosphere

Argon is used to make steel, and in welding to create a protective, inert atmosphere around metals. It's in many types of light bulbs, and surgeons use argon lasers in eye surgery and to destroy cancer cells. Neon signs containing argon glow blue.

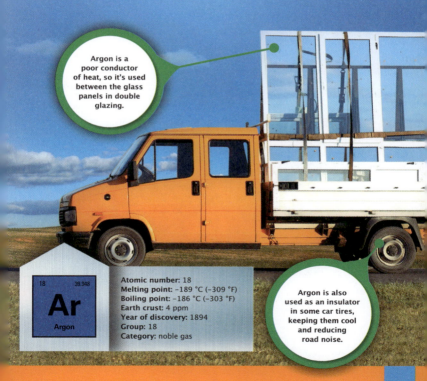

Argon is a poor conductor of heat, so it's used between the glass panels in double glazing.

Ar — Argon
18   39.948

Atomic number: 18
Melting point: −189 °C (−309 °F)
Boiling point: −186 °C (−303 °F)
Earth crust: 4 ppm
Year of discovery: 1894
Group: 18
Category: noble gas

Argon is also used as an insulator in some car tires, keeping them cool and reducing road noise.

Chapter 3: Period 4: Potassium to Krypton

Potassium

Potassium starts Period 4, with four energy shells. Like the other alkali metals in Group 1, it has one electron in its outer energy shell, so it's very reactive. Potassium would float on water—but it explodes first! It can even burn through ice.

Named After a Pot

Potassium is a silvery-gray metal, as soft as sticky putty. It was first isolated from potash ("pot-ash"), which is made from wood ash soaked in water in a pot and is used to make soaps and dyes. In 1807, Humphry Davy passed an electric current through potash and got metal drops that burned with a lilac flame on water. He called it potassium, after the kitchen pot.

We get our potassium from foods like meat and fish, nuts, raisins, bananas, Brussels sprouts, and chocolate.

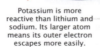

Potassium is more reactive than lithium and sodium. Its larger atom means its outer electron escapes more easily.

Nerve cells send messages by pumping potassium and sodium ions across membranes.

Atomic number: 19
Melting point: 64 °C (146 °F)
Boiling point: 759 °C (1,398 °F)
Earth crust: 22,774 ppm
Year of discovery: 1807
Group: 1
Category: alkali metal

DID YOU KNOW? A truckload of bananas has enough radioactive potassium-40 to set off a radiation detector. But eating bananas is perfectly safe!

Gunpowder and Fertilizer

Potassium is the seventh most abundant metal in Earth's crust. Its compounds have been known for centuries. Saltpeter (potassium nitrate) was used to make gunpowder in 9th-century China. Potassium salts are a natural fertilizer—traditionally extracted from guano (bird or bat poop) or scraped out of toilets!

Potassium can be extracted from deposits of minerals like sylvite, left by sea and lake evaporation.

A balanced diet contains potassium-rich foods. Potassium keeps cells healthy, controls fluid levels, and makes our nerves and muscles work.

Too little potassium can cause muscle cramps, but too much can cause diarrhea.

51

Calcium

Pure calcium is a soft, silvery-white metal. It is very reactive and forms a dull gray coating in the air. It's essential to all living things, especially for building hard skeletons and shells.

Mending and Building

Calcium is the fifth most common element in Earth's crust. It is found in rocky deposits like limestone and gypsum. Limestone (calcium carbonate) has been used as building stone for thousands of years, while gypsum (calcium sulfate) is used as plaster of Paris, for plastering walls or mending bones.

People made the Uffington White Horse in England 3,000 years ago by clearing away soil to show the chalk—a type of fine, soft limestone—underneath.

Rainwater seeps through rock into caves and evaporates. It leaves calcium carbonate behind as stalagmites and stalactites.

Limescale

Tap water is purified rainwater that has run through ground and rocks. Water from areas with limestone rocks picks up more dissolved calcium and magnesium ions, and we say it is "hard." Hard drinking water gives us extra minerals, but it makes annoying limescale: the chalky calcium carbonate that crusts around faucets and shower heads.

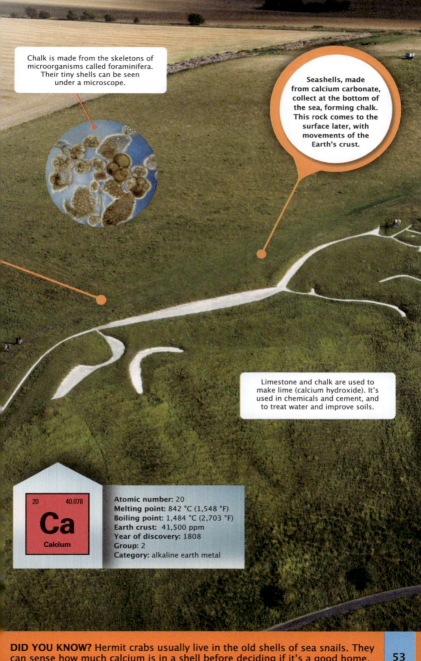

Chalk is made from the skeletons of microorganisms called foraminifera. Their tiny shells can be seen under a microscope.

Seashells, made from calcium carbonate, collect at the bottom of the sea, forming chalk. This rock comes to the surface later, with movements of the Earth's crust.

Limestone and chalk are used to make lime (calcium hydroxide). It's used in chemicals and cement, and to treat water and improve soils.

Ca — Calcium — 20 — 40.078

Atomic number: 20
Melting point: 842 °C (1,548 °F)
Boiling point: 1,484 °C (2,703 °F)
Earth crust: 41,500 ppm
Year of discovery: 1808
Group: 2
Category: alkaline earth metal

DID YOU KNOW? Hermit crabs usually live in the old shells of sea snails. They can sense how much calcium is in a shell before deciding if it's a good home.

Scandium

Scandium is the first transition metal in the Periodic Table, and the first rare earth metal of Group 3. The silvery metal was first found in Sweden and is named after Scandinavia.

Scandium alloys are used in bicycle frames, sports equipment, and more. A scandium–aluminum alloy has a melting point 800 °C (1,472 °F).

Atomic number: 21
Melting point: 1,541 °C (2,806 °F)
Boiling Point: 2,836 °C (5,137 °F)
Earth crust: trace amount
Year of discovery: 1879
Group: 3
Category: transition metal

Worth More Than Gold

Scandium is found as scandium oxide in small amounts around the world, but it's more common on the Moon than on Earth. It's so difficult to separate from its oxide that it's more valuable than gold.

Titanium

Titanium is the ninth most abundant element on Earth. Pure titanium is a shiny metal, but 95 percent of all we use is the brilliant white pigment titanium dioxide.

An electric current anodizes titanium, or gives it a protective coating of oxides. Anodized titanium is also decorative.

Superstrong

Titanium is named after the Titans of Greek myths. The metal is as strong as steel, but very light. It's mixed with aluminum to make lightweight, temperature-resistant alloys used in spacecraft and sports and medical equipment.

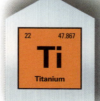

Atomic number: 22
Melting point: 1,670 °C (3,038 °F)
Boiling point: 3,287 °C (5,949 °F)
Earth crust: 4,136 ppm
Year of discovery: 1791
Group: 4
Category: transition metal

DID YOU KNOW? Spain's Guggenheim Museum is protected by 33,000 tiles of anti-corrosion titanium sheet, guaranteed for over 100 years.

Vanadium

Vanadium is a silvery-gray metal that is malleable (can be shaped without breaking) and is mainly used as an alloy to strengthen steel. Vanadium pentoxide is an important catalyst for sulfuric acid production.

Vanadium also makes beautiful crystals, but its compounds can be toxic. It's named after Freya, the Norse goddess of beauty.

Possible Diabetes Drug

People need tiny traces of vanadium. It affects cell growth and enzyme function. Research suggests it could help control sugar levels in diabetics.

Sea creatures called sea squirts store vanadium until it's up to 10 million times more concentrated in their bodies than in seawater.

Accumulated vanadium may protect sea squirts from predators by making them taste bad.

23 50.9415
V
Vanadium

Atomic number: 23
Melting point: 1,910 °C (3,470 °F)
Boiling point: 3,407 °C (6,165 °F)
Earth crust: 138 ppm
Year of discovery: 1801
Group: 5
Category: transition metal

Chromium

Chromium is a hard, silvery-blue metal with a very high melting point. It's used in chromium plating and to harden steel and make stainless steel and other alloys.

Rainbow Compounds

Like other transition metals, chromium forms ions with different charges (see pages 18–19). It gives up two electrons to make Cr^{2+}, and it gives up three electrons to make Cr^{3+}. These oxidation states produce a range of stunning hues. The name chromium means "color."

School buses in the U.S. are painted National School Bus Chrome yellow. The original paint contained lead chromate; both lead and chromium are toxic. It's now replaced with safer pigments.

Anything from motorbikes to plastic bathroom fittings can be given a mirrorlike, shiny coating with chromium plating.

Atomic number: 24
Melting point: 1,907 °C (3,465 °F)
Boiling point: 2,671 °C (4,840 °F)
Earth crust: 135 ppm
Year of discovery: 1798
Group: 6
Category: transition metal

Manganese

Manganese is a hard, brittle, silvery metal. Don't confuse it with magnesium (element number 12). They're both named after Magnesia—the area in Greece where they were first discovered.

Prison Bars and Batteries

An alloy of steel with just 1 percent manganese is stronger than steel on its own. Adding 13 percent makes superstrong manganese steel, used in train tracks, safes, and prison bars. Drink cans don't corrode because the aluminum alloy contains manganese. It's also used to make lithium-ion batteries.

> We wouldn't be here without manganese. It is an essential part of a plant enzyme that breaks water into oxygen in photosynthesis.

> Manganese is essential for life. We get it from nuts, bran, and whole grains, and we need it for strong bones and a healthy metabolism.

> In areas where soil has low levels of manganese, farmers use fertilizers and food supplements for grazing animals.

25 **54.93804**
Mn
Manganese

Atomic number: 25
Melting point: 1,246 °C (2,275 °F)
Boiling point: 2,061 °C (3,742 °F)
Earth crust: 774 ppm
Year of discovery: 1774
Group: 7
Category: transition metal

DID YOU KNOW? Manganese-rich nodules found on deep-sea beds grow around ancient shark teeth, like pearls forming around grains of sand.

Iron

Iron is essential to life and industry. People have been turning it into objects since prehistoric times. It makes up 90 percent of all the metal we refine, or purify.

> Iron ore is heated with coke (carbon) and limestone (calcium carbonate) in a blast furnace, and the molten iron poured off. This process is smelting.

Better as Steel

Most refined iron is used to produce steel—an alloy of iron and carbon. Steel is much stronger than iron and is used in everything from bicycle chains to bridges. In 2023, world crude steel production was 1,888 million tonnes (1,858 million tons), and the industry recycles about 30 percent of steel per year.

Iron and steel have a drawback. They react with oxygen to make iron oxide. This is familiar red, flaky rust, which weakens the metal.

Magnetic

Iron is magnetic, which means magnets attract it, and it can also make magnets. The only other elements that are magnetic at room temperature are cobalt and nickel. Steel contains iron, so it's magnetic too. We use magnets for many things, from fridge magnets to computers.

A lodestone can pick up steel paper clips because it's made of the magnetic iron ore magnetite.

DID YOU KNOW? The Eiffel Tower contains 7,300 tonnes (8,045 tons) of a construction iron called puddling iron. It expands 15 cm (6 in) in hot weather.

Cobalt

Cobalt is a hard, magnetic, silvery-blue metal. It's found combined in ores with other transition metals. People have used its bright blue compounds in glass and pottery for thousands of years.

Superalloys and Magnets

A very high melting point means cobalt makes superalloys with other metals. The alloys stay strong in intense heat, so they work well in engines. Cobalt also makes powerful magnets, such as "alnico" magnets made with aluminum and nickel, which stay magnetic at high temperatures.

This statue with a cobalt blue glass cap was made for the tomb of the Egyptian king Tutankhamun, who died in 1323 BCE.

Cobalt chloride is blue, but water turns it pink—it's used to show where conditions are damp.

Atomic number: 27
Melting point: 1,495 °C (2,723 °F)
Boiling point: 2,927 °C (5,301 °F)
Earth crust: 26.6 ppm
Year of discovery: 1739
Group: 9
Category: transition metal

DID YOU KNOW? You can write a secret letter with cobalt chloride solution. The invisible ink appears when the writing paper is heated.

Nickel

Nickel is a silvery metal that doesn't corrode, even at high temperatures. Like cobalt, it makes "superalloys" with other metals.

It's thought iron accounts for 85 percent of Earth's inner core, while nickel makes up around 10 percent. The temperature of the inner core is 5,500 °C (9,932 °F).

Heat Strengthening

About half of the nickel produced is alloyed with iron and chromium to make stainless steel. With aluminum, nickel can form an alloy six times stronger than stainless steel. There is increasing demand for nickel, for use in lithium-ion batteries for electric cars.

Nickel superalloys are in heat-resistant objects, from toasters to plane engines.

Superstrong nickel–aluminum alloys get even stronger as they get hotter.

Ni — Nickel
28   58.6934

Atomic number: 28
Melting point: 1,455 °C (2,651 °F)
Boiling point: 2,913 °C (5,275 °F)
Earth crust: 26.6 ppm
Year of discovery: 1751
Group: 10
Category: transition metal

61

Copper

Copper is a soft, red-gold metal, found as ores and pure copper nuggets. It was worked in ancient times—beads have been found from 10,000 years ago. The Romans mined copper in Cyprus, naming it after the island.

Perfect for Wiring

Copper is ductile—that is, it can be drawn into wires—and it conducts electricity and heat well, so it's widely used in electrical equipment. In developed countries, around 175 kg (386 lbs) of copper is in use for every person. Around a third of what is used worldwide is recycled.

When copper reacts with air, it makes green compounds—verdigris—which stop the metal from corroding more. Copper jewelry can stain skin green!

Around 3500 BCE, people started adding tin to make copper harder. The new alloy made better tools than stone, and better armor than copper. The Bronze Age had begun.

Atomic number: 29
Melting point: 1,085 °C (1,984 °F)
Boiling point: 2,560 °C (4,640 °F)
Earth crust: 27 ppm
Year of discovery: prehistory
Group: 11
Category: transition metal

DID YOU KNOW? Copper and zinc pair up to make brass—the alloy used in brass instruments and the etched brass rubbing plates on ancient tombs.

Zinc

Zinc is a bluish-silver metal, known long before it was officially discovered. A medieval smelting workshop in Zawar, Rajasthan, India, left so much waste, we can guess it refined more than a million tonnes (1,102,311 tons) of zinc.

Galvanizing

Galvanizing gives metals a rust-resistant coating. They are coated with zinc, either by dipping into hot liquid zinc, or by electrolysis—an electric current running through a solution of dissolved zinc. Coating by electrolysis is called electroplating. Tableware and jewelry are electroplated with nickel silver—an alloy of zinc, nickel, and copper.

Large steel structures are dipped into a bath of pure, melted zinc. Every year, more than 11 million tonnes (12,125,400 tons) of zinc is produced from ores worldwide.

Zinc is a useful roofing material. In the 19th century, Baron Haussmann modernized Paris, using zinc for the rooftops. More than 80 percent of Parisian roofs are now zinc.

Zinc tarnishes in air, creating an oxidized layer—a patina—that protects the metal underneath from corrosion.

Atomic number: 30
Melting point: 420 °C (787 °F)
Boiling point: 907 °C (1,665 °F)
Earth crust: 72 ppm
Year of discovery: 1746
Group: 12
Category: transition metal

63

Gallium

In his Periodic Table, Dmitri Mendeleev left a space under aluminum for an unknown element that he called "eka-aluminum." Six years later, Frenchman Paul-Émile Lecoq de Boisbaudran found a metal that fit. He named it gallium.

Semiconducting Compounds

Gallium is a soft, silver-white metal, found in tiny amounts in minerals like bauxite. It's made as a byproduct of aluminum and zinc refining. Gallium arsenide and gallium nitride are semiconductors—they sometimes conduct electricity—and they are used in chips, LED lights, mobile phones, pressure sensors, and Blu-ray technology.

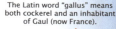

Gallium's melting point is so low, it melts in your hand. It gets denser as it melts, so—like ice and water—solid gallium floats on liquid gallium.

Gallium's boiling point is so high, it can be used to measure very high temperatures.

The Latin word "gallus" means both cockerel and an inhabitant of Gaul (now France).

Atomic number: 31
Melting point: 30 °C (86 °F)
Boiling point: 2,229 °C (4,044 °F)
Earth crust: 16 ppm
Year of discovery: 1875
Group: 13
Category: post-transition metal

DID YOU KNOW? Lecoq named gallium after "Gallia," the Latin word for France, but it's also a clever pun on his own name—"le coq" means rooster or cockerel.

Germanium

Mendeleev left another space next to "eka-aluminum" in his Periodic Table, which he called "eka-silicon." Clemens Winkler later discovered a brittle, silvery-gray element with the right properties for "eka-silicon." He named it germanium after his country, Germany.

Radar Breakthrough

Trace amounts of germanium are found in zinc ores and other minerals. The element is a metalloid—it looks like a metal and it sometimes conducts electricity. It was first used in diodes and transistors in World War II. It's now usually replaced by silicon as a semiconductor.

Germanium transistor radios replaced vacuum tube radios like this.

An important modern use of germanium is in fiber optic cables. It makes the fibers more efficient because the light can't escape.

Germanium is a good carrier of light. It has found new uses because of its interesting optical properties.

32   72.64
Ge
Germanium

Atomic number: 32
Melting point: 938 °C (1,721 °F)
Boiling point: 2,833 °C (5,131 °F)
Earth crust: 1 ppm
Year of discovery: 1886
Group: 14
Category: metalloid

Arsenic

Pure arsenic has three allotropes: yellow nonmetals, black nonmetals, and a gray metal-like form. When it's heated it doesn't melt—it vaporizes straight to gas (sublimation). Prawns contain surprisingly high levels of a safe arsenic compound.

Orpiment is an arsenic sulfide mineral used to represent gold in ancient Egyptian art.

Toxic but Useful

Arsenic has been used to poison pests—and people—for centuries. It is toxic to the liver and causes cancer although it's now used in a treatment for leukemia (blood cancer). It's also an important doping agent in electronics—helping current to flow in semiconductors.

Arsenic was found in the body of Otzi the Iceman who lived between 3350 and 3105 BCE. Arsenic is a byproduct of copper refining, so perhaps Otzi was a coppersmith.

33 74.922
As
Arsenic

Atomic number: 33
Melting point: 616 °C (1,141 °F)
Boiling point: 616 °C (1,141 °F)
Earth crust: 2.5 ppm
Year of discovery: around 1250
Group: 15
Category: metalloid

DID YOU KNOW? In years 1837 and 1838 alone, England and Wales had 186 repor of arsenic-related deaths. A few were murders, but accidental death was common.

Selenium

Selenium, meaning "Moon," is a photoconductor—long chains of selenium atoms will conduct electricity when exposed to light. That makes it very useful in solar panels and photocopiers. It's also an important glass additive.

Essentially Smelly

Selenium is an essential trace element. Too little is bad, but too much can make sweat and breath garlicky. In very high doses it can be fatal. A selenium compound is the stinkiest part of skunk smell and is one of the worst-smelling chemicals ever.

Plants bioaccumulate (store and concentrate) selenium from soil, so crops grown on soil with the right levels are a good food source.

Solar cells absorb sunlight to make electricity. Selenium is part of CIGS (copper indium gallium selenide) solar cells.

Selenium increases the efficiency of solar panels made of a cadmium–telluride semiconductor.

Atomic number: 34
Melting point: 221 °C (429 °F)
Boiling point: 685 °C (1,265 °F)
Earth crust: trace amount
Year of discovery: 1817
Group: 16
Category: nonmetal

67

Bromine

Bromine is a toxic, smelly, deep-red, oily liquid, and its name means "stench." It's one of only two elements that are liquid at room temperature and pressure. It is volatile, giving off harmful orange fumes.

Difficult to Replace

Bromine has been used in lots of things, including pesticides, photography, fire extinguishers, and leaded fuels. Many uses were stopped because of environmental harm—but bromine is still used in plastics and to make life-saving drugs, where alternatives are hard to find.

Sea snails make protective mucus containing the toxic bromine compound. This was once used to make a rich purple dye by boiling snail glands for several days!

In 1st-century Rome, 0.5 kg (1 lb) of purple dye was worth three times its weight in gold. Only rich people could wear clothes dyed with the compound.

35	79.904
Br	
Bromine	

Atomic number: 35
Melting point: −7 °C (19 °F)
Boiling point: 59 °C (138 °F)
Earth crust: 1 ppm
Year of discovery: 1826
Group: 17
Category: halogen

Krypton

Krypton is the final element in Period 4—it has a full outer energy shell containing eight electrons. It's a rare gas that reacts only with fluorine, discovered when William Ramsay looked for unknown elements to join argon in a whole new Periodic Table Group.

Hidden in Lights and Lasers

Krypton is invisible, with no color, smell, or taste—its name means "hidden." In fiction, it was the inspiration for Superman's home planet, Krypton. It's used in lights, from flashlights and photographic flashbulbs to airport runway lights. Krypton fluoride lasers produce intense ultraviolet light that can burn a hole through walls!

High-powered krypton fluoride lasers are used in eye surgery and also in electronics and research into nuclear fusion energy.

Krypton is used to produce different colors, especially red and bright yellow, in laser light shows.

Atomic number: 36
Melting point: −157 °C (−251 °F)
Boiling point: −153 °C (−244 °F)
Earth crust: trace amounts
Year of discovery: 1898
Group: 18
Category: noble gas

DID YOU KNOW? Between 1960 and 1983, the standard length of 1 m (3 ft) was based on 1,650,763.73 wavelengths of light emitted by krypton-86.

69

Chapter 4: Period 5: Rubidium to Xenon

Rubidium

Period 5 begins with rubidium. The soft, silvery metal is even more reactive than the alkali metals above it in Group 1. It catches fire in air and explodes in water, so is stored under oil or in an inert gas.

Physics Research

At low temperatures of almost absolute zero, rubidium becomes a superfluid (meaning it flows with almost no friction), with properties that could help scientists study space. It is slightly radioactive and is used in medicine to find tumors and to show the workings of the heart.

Scientists have created a superfluid of 2,000 rubidium atoms that behave like a single atom at very cold temperatures.

Early chemists couldn't understand why the pebbles from the mineral lepidolite frothed out on hot coals. It was because the mineral contains very reactive rubidium.

Rb Rubidium
37   85.4678

Atomic number: 37
Melting point: 39 °C (103 °F)
Boiling point: 688 °C (1,270 °F)
Earth crust: 90 ppm
Year of discovery: 1861
Group: 1
Category: alkali metal

Strontium

Like the other alkaline earth metals in Group 2, strontium is a reactive, soft, silvery metal. It's quite abundant in Earth's crust. It is essential to some marine animals for building their shells.

Nuclear Hazard and Help

The isotope strontium-90 is used in nuclear reactors. Reactor leaks are hazardous, as strontium can enter bones just like calcium and cause cancer. However, non-radioactive strontium is used to treat cancer and osteoporosis (brittle bones)—and to make the most accurate atomic clock.

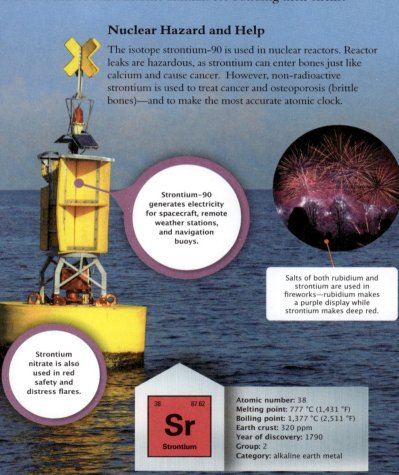

Strontium-90 generates electricity for spacecraft, remote weather stations, and navigation buoys.

Salts of both rubidium and strontium are used in fireworks—rubidium makes a purple display while strontium makes deep red.

Strontium nitrate is also used in red safety and distress flares.

Sr — Strontium
- 38
- 87.62

Atomic number: 38
Melting point: 777 °C (1,431 °F)
Boiling point: 1,377 °C (2,511 °F)
Earth crust: 320 ppm
Year of discovery: 1790
Group: 2
Category: alkaline earth metal

DID YOU KNOW? Archaeologists think Roman gladiators ate a largely plant-based diet because of the high levels of strontium in the ancient bones.

Yttrium to Technetium

Yttrium, zirconium, and niobium are all chemically like the elements below them in their Groups. This made it hard for chemists to isolate yttrium from lanthanides, and zirconium from hafnium, and niobium from tantalum. Pure zirconium wasn't made until 1925.

> Yttrium, zirconium, and niobium alloys are superconductors—they conduct without losing heat. They make magnets used in MRI scanners.

Atomic number: 39
Melting point: 1,522 °C (1,522 °F)
Boiling point: 3,345 °C (6,053 °F)
Earth crust: 33 ppm
Year of discovery: 1794
Group: 3
Category: transition metal

Atomic number: 40
Melting point: 1,854 °C (3,369 °F)
Boiling point: 4,406 °C (7,963 °F)
Earth crust: 132 ppm
Year of discovery: 1789
Group: 4
Category: transition metal

Atomic number: 41
Melting point: 2,477 °C (4,491 °F)
Boiling point: 4,741 °C (8,566 °F)
Earth crust: 8 ppm
Year of discovery: 1801
Group: 5
Category: transition metal

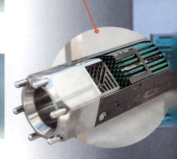

The tubes around nuclear reactor rods are made of zirconium, which lets neutrons through. Zirconium is also used in antiperspirants.

Molybdenum and Technetium

Molybdenum is an essential element for plants and animals. It's found in nitrogenase—an enzyme in bacteria that makes nitrogen available to green plants. Technetium is the lightest radioactive element. There's hardly any in Earth's crust. It's made artificially in nuclear power plants, where it's a byproduct of uranium fission.

As well as MRI scanners, superconducting magnets are used in particle accelerators and equipment for studying atoms.

Technetium is a medical imaging agent. It highlights medical issues, which are detected by the MRI scanner.

Tc — Technetium — 43 (98)

Atomic number: 43
Melting point: 2,157 °C (3,915 °F)
Boiling point: 4,262 °C (4,262 °F)
Earth crust: trace amount
Year of discovery: 1937
Group: 7
Category: transition metal

Mo — Molybdenum — 42 95.96

Atomic number: 42
Melting point: 2,622 °C (4,752 °F)
Boiling point: 4,639 °C (8,382 °F)
Earth crust: 1 ppm
Year of discovery: 1781
Group: 6
Category: transition metal

DID YOU KNOW? Eighty percent of nuclear medical imaging uses technetium to diagnose medical problems.

Ruthenium

One of the rarest metals on Earth, ruthenium is a byproduct of nickel refining. Its name comes from the Latin name for Russia.

Ruthenium catalysts build hydrocarbon compounds. They're used in industrial processes—and to make scented candle wax.

Atomic number: 44
Melting point: 2,333 °C (4,231 °F)
Boiling point: 4,147 °C (7,497 °F)
Earth crust: trace amount
Year of discovery: 1844
Group: 8
Category: transition metal

Ruthenium Sponge

Ruthenium is very reactive, and it is used as a catalyst for making ammonia and acetic acid. Most ruthenium is used in electronics. It's alloyed with platinum and palladium in electrical contacts, and a red ruthenium compound is used in solar cells.

Rhodium

Rhodium is very expensive, but it's an important catalyst in the chemical industry. Eighty percent of its use is in catalytic converters in cars.

Rarest of All

Rhodium is the rarest of all non-radioactive metals. It's made as a byproduct of copper and nickel refining—just 30 tonnes (33 tons) per year is produced globally. As well as in catalysts, it's used in optical fibers, electrical contacts, and headlight reflectors.

Rhodium catalysts produce thousands of tons per year of menthol—the flavoring used in chewing gum.

Atomic number: 45
Melting point: 1,963 °C (3,565 °F)
Boiling point: 3,695 °C (6,683 °F)
Earth crust: trace amount
Year of discovery: 1803
Group: 9
Category: transition metal

DID YOU KNOW? In 1979, Paul McCartney was awarded a rhodium-plated disc when he was named "all-time best-selling songwriter and recording artist."

Palladium

> Palladium, rhodium, and platinum are used in catalytic converters, removing harmful emissions from car exhausts.

Ruthenium, rhodium, and palladium—with osmium, iridium, and platinum—are the Platinum Group Metals (PGMs). They have similar chemical properties and appear together in minerals and river sands. They are all rare and expensive, and they make good catalysts. PGMs will be increasingly important in batteries and hydrogen fuel cells as green technology improves.

Organic Synthesis

Palladium is an important industrial catalyst, used in making hydrocarbons (carbon-hydrogen compounds) and in building other organic molecules.

> Dentists use palladium in fillings and crowns. It's also used in jewelry.

> The precious metals are recycled from catalytic converters in old car exhausts.

Pd
Palladium
46   106.42

Atomic number: 46
Melting point: 1,555 °C (2,831 °F)
Boiling point: 2,963 °C (5,365 °F)
Earth crust: trace amount
Year of discovery: 1803
Group: 10
Category: transition metal

75

Silver

Silver is one of eight precious metals, along with gold and the Platinum Group Metals. Silver is found pure and in ores, and people have been mining it and making coins and jewelry since around 3000 BCE.

> Modern mirrors have a thin layer of silver, making a reflective layer on the back of a sheet of glass.

Modern Technology

Silver is an excellent electrical conductor, so it's used in solders, electrical contacts, batteries, and digital photography. Silver is in printed circuits and enables you to use your phone touchscreen with gloves on. Silver is also antibacterial, so tiny silver nanoparticles kill the bacteria that make your socks smelly.

Photochromic lenses go dark in sunshine because they contain light-sensitive silver chloride.

Photographic Film

Non-digital photography uses light-sensitive silver salts. When the camera snaps a picture, light falls on a silver bromide layer on the photographic film. It starts a reaction—the silver and bromide ions become silver and bromine atoms. More silver atoms are produced in areas that received more light. When the film is developed, the silver shows up black in the negative of the photograph.

Film is developed in a dark room with red light to stop over-exposure to other wavelengths.

DID YOU KNOW? Silver makes it rain—silver iodide is sometimes dropped from planes to make clouds form ice crystals, and rain. It's called cloud seeding.

Copper is more reactive than silver and so displaces it in a silver nitrate solution. The solution turns blue, and silver crystals form.

Silver is the best reflector of light. Reflected light creates an image in the glass.

Silver reacts with sulfur in the air—the surface tarnishes with dark, dull silver sulfide. Polishing silver keeps it shiny!

Ag — Silver
47   107.8682

Atomic number: 47
Melting point: 962 °C (1,763 °F)
Boiling point: 2,162 °C (3,924 °F)
Earth crust: trace amount
Year of discovery: prehistoric
Group: 11
Category: transition metal

77

Cadmium

Cadmium is a silvery metal with a blue tinge. It's similar to zinc (number 30) and found with zinc ores. It can cause cancer, damage bones, and harm developing embryos—and before this was known, metal workers were dangerously exposed to it.

Use with Care

Cadmium is now carefully controlled in uses such as electroplating aircraft parts, and as a neutron-absorber in nuclear reactor rods. It's used in rechargeable nickel-cadmium batteries, which are being phased out, but still could be important in future electric vehicles.

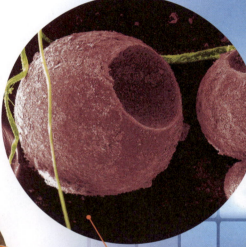

Tiny quantum dots are nanoparticles of cadmium salts that are a new class of semiconductors in electronics.

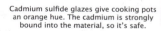

Cadmium sulfide glazes give cooking pots an orange hue. The cadmium is strongly bound into the material, so it's safe.

48　112.414
Cd
Cadmium

Atomic number: 48
Melting point: 321 °C (610 °F)
Boiling point: 767 °C (1,413 °F)
Earth crust: trace amount
Year of discovery: 1817
Group: 12
Category: transition metal

DID YOU KNOW? A terrible bone disease due to cadmium-contaminated rice and drinking water in Japan in the 20th century was descriptively called "Ouch Ouch!"

Indium

Indium is a very soft, shiny, malleable metal with a low melting point. Like cadmium, it's produced as a byproduct of zinc refining and is toxic if breathed in or eaten. It's quite rare and expensive.

Useful Properties

Indium stays workable at low temperatures, so it's used in equipment exposed to extreme cold. Tiny amounts strengthen gold alloys. Indium sticks to itself and other metals, so it makes a good solder. It sticks to glass to give a mirror finish to windows of tall buildings, reflecting infrared light.

Indium has low friction and has been used to coat ball bearings in Formula 1 racing cars.

Indium tin oxide (ITO) is transparent and conductive. It is used in electronics, including in holographic displays.

Indium allows electric current and light to flow across your phone or computer screen.

49   114.818
In
Indium

Atomic number: 49
Melting point: 157 °C (314 °F)
Boiling point: 2,027 °C (3,681 °F)
Earth crust: trace amount
Year of discovery: 1863
Group: 13
Category: post-transition metal

Tin

Tin is a soft, malleable, silvery metal. It's found mainly in the "tin belt" of China, Thailand, and Indonesia, and was mined in China from around 700 BCE. The symbol, Sn, comes from its Latin name, stannum.

Many Uses

Tin salts are used in the chemicals, dyes, and ceramics industries, in fire retardants, and to make conductive coatings on glass. Window glass is made by floating molten glass on molten tin—the float glass process. Tin is nontoxic, but organotins—compounds with organic chemicals—can be poisonous. Tin compounds in paints designed for boats killed sea life and have been banned.

The "white" allotrope of tin is the familiar, shiny metal traditionally used in church organ pipes.

Alloys

Tin content in alloys hardens the other metals and lowers their melting points. Its alloy with copper—bronze—defines the Bronze Age of ancient history. With lead, tin makes a good solder for joining metals. Niobium-tin alloy is used for superconducting magnets. Pewter is a bluish alloy, usually of tin, copper, and antimony.

The tin coating in steel cans stops food spoiling.

Gold-plated Oscar statuettes are made of a pewter called Britannia metal.

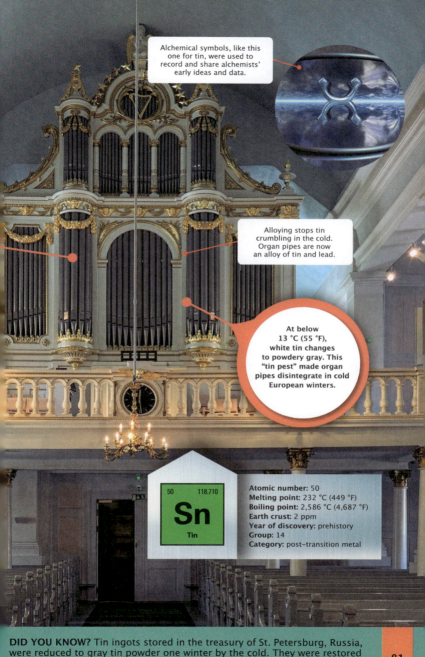

DID YOU KNOW? Tin ingots stored in the treasury of St. Petersburg, Russia, were reduced to gray tin powder one winter by the cold. They were restored to white tin by melting and recasting them.

Antimony

Antimony is a semimetal—the metallic form does not conduct electricity well, and so it's used in electronics to make semiconductor devices. It also has nonmetallic yellow, black, and white allotropes.

In the 1430s, Johann Gutenberg invented the printing press with type letters made of lead alloy hardened with antimony.

Medical Debate

Like arsenic in the same Group, antimony is toxic, yet people have used it for thousands of years. In the 17th century, European doctors argued bitterly about its benefits and drawbacks. Its early use as a laxative wasn't safe, but it's now used to treat leishmaniasis, a parasitic disease.

Atomic number: 51
Melting point: 631 °C (1,167 °F)
Boiling Point: 1,587 °C (2,889 °F)
Earth crust: trace amount
Year of discovery: prehistory
Group: 15
Category: metalloid

Tellurium

Tellurium is a semi-metal, usually in the form of a dark gray powder. Its name comes from "Tellus," the Latin word for Earth.

The compound cadmium telluride is used to capture the Sun's energy in very efficient, thin film solar cells.

Vampire Connections

Tellurium was first discovered in Transylvania, and—if eaten—it makes breath smell disgustingly garlicky. It's also produced from the anode slime produced in copper refining. Fortunately, tellurium has its good side. It's used to improve stainless steel and lead alloys, as a catalyst in oil refining, and in laser optics and semiconductors.

Atomic number: 52
Melting point: 450 °C (841 °F)
Boiling point: 988 °C (1,810 °F)
Earth crust: trace amount
Year of discovery: 1783
Group: 16
Category: metalloid

DID YOU KNOW? Tellurium is one of the few elements that make compound with gold. Telluride, Colorado, is named after gold telluride minerals.

Iodine

Iodine is a nonmetal. Like the other halogens in Group 17, it only needs one electron to fill up its outer energy shell, making it very reactive.

> Iodine is essential to life. Tadpoles kept in water without iodine never turn into frogs.

The Purple One

Iodine is named after the Greek word for "violet." It's a black, crystalline solid that dissolves to make brown or purple solutions. When it's heated, the solid doesn't melt, it sublimes—turns directly into a purple vapor. Iodine is used as a disinfectant, in water purification tablets, and as a weird, dramatic red antiseptic painted onto skin cuts and grazes.

> In humans, lack of iodine affects the thyroid gland, causing goiter (neck swelling). Table salt is fortified with iodine.

Many species of seaweed take in iodine from seawater. Seaweed is a good food source.

53	126.9044
I	
Iodine	

Atomic number: 53
Melting point: 114 °C (237 °F)
Boiling point: 184 °C (364 °F)
Earth crust: 1 ppm
Year of discovery: 1811
Group: 17
Category: halogen

Xenon

The last element in Period 5, xenon, was discovered in 1898 by William Ramsay and Morris Travers, at the end of a four-year search for the noble gases of Group 18. It was discovered in a sample of krypton isolated from liquid air.

Noble Rarity

Xenon is the rarest gas in the atmosphere, and only around 60 tonnes (66 tons) per year is commercially produced. Around 15 percent is used as an anesthetic. It's also used in car headlights, camera flashbulbs, food hygiene, sunbed lamps, and medical imaging.

Xenon is produced at temperatures around −173 °C (−279 °F) in cryogenic air separation plants.

Xenon ion propulsion engines keep satellites in orbit. The engine was the first non-chemical propulsion system used in spacecraft.

Not So Inert

Group 18 elements were named "inert gases" because they seemed totally unreactive. But in 1962, chemist Neil Bartlett made a xenon compound, proving that they will react in some circumstances. More than 100 xenon compounds, plus compounds of other noble gases, have now been made.

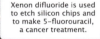

Xenon difluoride is used to etch silicon chips and to make 5-fluorouracil, a cancer treatment.

DID YOU KNOW? Under pressure, xenon will form a bright blue solid.

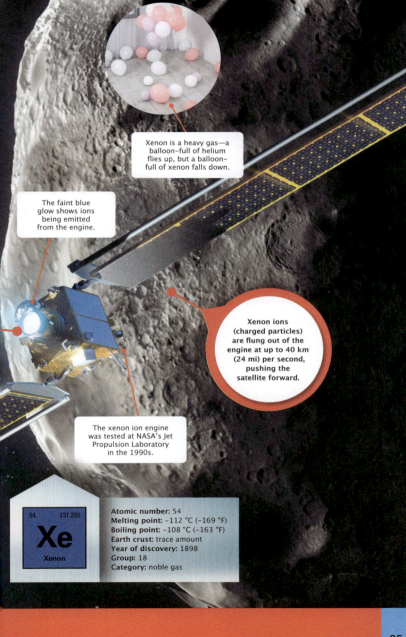

Chapter 5: Period 6: Cesium to Radon

Cesium

Cesium is the first element in Period 6. It's a big atom with six energy shells and only one outer electron. That electron escapes so easily that cesium is probably the most reactive element of all!

Explosive and Accurate

Cesium is dangerously explosive, but it's used in atomic clocks, which are accurate to one second in 158 million years and are used in phone networks and satellites to keep us all to the same time. Cesium is also used in glass, catalysts, vacuum tubes, radiation monitoring equipment, and drilling fluids.

An atomic clock uses just 1 gram (0.035 oz) per year of cesium. Its "tick" is measured by an electron bouncing between energy levels in the atom.

Cesium's gold hue is due to traces of oxygen.

Atomic number: 55
Melting point: 29 °C (83 °F)
Boiling point: 671 °C (1,240 °F)
Earth crust: 3 ppm
Year of discovery: 1860
Group: 1
Category: alkali metals

DID YOU KNOW? The melting point of cesium is so low that on a warm day it will melt, and resolidify as the temperature drops at night.

Barium

Barium is a soft, reactive, silvery metal that's incredibly toxic. Just 1g can kill a person. Its compounds are also toxic and have been used in pesticides.

Heavyweight

"Barys" means heavy—and barium and its compounds are very heavy. Barite (barium sulfate) is used in oil wells as a weighting agent in drilling, and in hospitals, where the dense material scatters X-rays in radiography. Barium carbonate gives shine in glass-making, and barium nitrate makes fireworks green.

Some phytoplankton store barium. As they die, they sink. Barite levels in mud can tell scientists how much life the ocean has supported over time.

A barium "meal" is a suspension of barium sulfate in a liquid. It's swallowed so doctors can diagnose problems in the digestive system through X-ray imaging.

Most barium salts are poisonous, but barium sulphate is inert and so the suspension passes harmlessly through the body.

Ba — Barium
56 — 137.327

Atomic number: 56
Melting point: 727 °C (1,341 °F)
Boiling point: 1,845 °C (3,353 °F)
Earth crust: 456 ppm
Year of discovery: 1808
Group: 2
Category: alkaline earth metals

Lanthanum

Lanthanum begins the lanthanide series—15 similar metals that are displayed outside of the Periodic Table so it can fit on the page. The lanthanides (numbers 57–71), scandium (number 21), and yttrium (number 39) are known as rare earth elements, but they're not rare—they're just difficult to separate out of their ores. They are very much in demand in the high-tech electronics industry.

Hidden

In 1839, Carl Gustav Mosander unexpectedly discovered lanthanum in a sample of cerium. He named it after the Greek work for "lie hidden." Its alloys are used to make steel less brittle, to store hydrogen fuels, and in catalysts and batteries.

Radioactive isotope, lanthanum-138 has a half-life (see page 120) of 100 billion years, so scientists use it to radio-date rock that's billions of years old.

Lanthanum oxide gives a bright, crystal effect to glass and is used in camera and telescope lenses.

Atomic number: 57
Melting point: 920 °C (1,688 °F)
Boiling point: 3,464 °C (6,267 °F)
Earth crust: 32 ppm
Year of discovery: 1839
Group: 3
Category: lanthanide

Cerium

Cerium is the most common lanthanide in Earth's crust and is almost as abundant as zinc. It's highly reactive, especially as a powder, but it makes very stable oxides.

Useful Oxides

Cerium oxide (ceria) is very hard, so it's good for grinding and polishing lenses. It makes vehicles less damaging to the environment—in catalytic converters it makes engines burn fuel more efficiently, and it reduces exhaust emissions from diesel fuels. It also helps cooking splatters slide off the inside of self-cleaning ovens.

Cerium is a silvery-gray metal. Its compounds include a red pigment, cerium sulfide.

Mischmetal alloy makes lighters spark and is used in ferrocerium fire sticks for lighting campfires. It is around 50 percent cerium and 20 percent lanthanum.

Cerium is pyrophoric—it sparks when struck against a hard surface. Apart from iron, no other element does this.

58   140.116
Ce
Cerium

Atomic number: 58
Melting point: 799 °C (1,470 °F)
Boiling point: 3,443 °C (6,229 °F)
Earth crust: 68 ppm
Year of discovery: 1803
Group: N/A
Category: lanthanide

DID YOU KNOW? Cerium dioxide is a rule breaker. It should have two oxygens for every cerium atom, but its surface has gaps where oxygen atoms should be.

Praseodymium

The lanthanides are very tangled! In 1841, Carl Mosander separated didymium from cerium and lanthanum, and named it as an element. Forty years later, didymium was found to be twin elements—praseodymium and neodymium.

Praseodymium and neodymium make didymium glass—used in welder's goggles.

Superstrong Alloy

Praseodymium is used with magnesium to make a very strong alloy for aircraft engines. Its alloys are also used in permanent magnets and in lighter flint mischmetal. Its salts give glass a strong yellow hue.

59 140.9076
Pr
Praseodymium

Atomic number: 59
Melting point: 931 °C (1,708 °F)
Boiling Point: 3,520 °C (6,368 °F)
Earth crust: 10 ppm
Year of discovery: 1885
Group: N/A
Category: lanthanide

Neodymium

Neodymium is used as a component in industrial laser cutting tools, and to color glass purple. Neodymium glass is used in sunbed booths, where it lets UV rays through but stops infrared rays.

Neodymium glass is in lasers used in eye surgery, skin treatments, and in laser pointers.

60 144.242
Nd
Neodymium

Atomic number: 60
Melting point: 1,016 °C (1,861 °F)
Boiling Point: 3,074 °C (5,565 °F)
Earth crust: 38 ppm
Year of discovery: 1885
Group: N/A
Category: lanthanide

Supermagnets

Neodymium makes powerful permanent magnets that can hold 1,000 times their own weight—10 times stronger than a normal iron magnet. An alloy of neodymium, iron, and boron (NIB) is used in electronic devices.

Promethium

Promethium saves the lives of heart patients. It's used in atomic batteries the size of fingernail to power pacemakers.

Promethium is the only radioactive lanthanide. It's named after Prometheus in Greek mythology.

Radioactive

Promethium's isotopes all have a half-life (see page 120) of less than 18 years, so Earth's original supply of promethium disappeared long ago. It's now produced in nuclear reactors and is used in research and in instruments to measure thickness. It can be made into luminous paint.

Atomic number: 61
Melting point: 1,042 °C (1,908 °F)
Boiling Point: 3,000 °C (5,432 °F)
Earth crust: none
Year of discovery: 1945
Group: N/A
Category: lanthanide

Samarium

Samarium is a good neutron absorber. It's used in nuclear reactor rods to control the chain reaction. It makes powerful, high-temperature magnets.

Atomic number: 62
Melting point: 1,072 °C (1,962 °F)
Boiling Point: 1,794 °C (3,261 °F)
Earth crust: 8 ppm
Year of discovery: 1879
Group: N/A
Category: lanthanide

Samarium magnets are used in electric guitar pickups—they pick up the string vibration and turn it into an electric signal.

DID YOU KNOW? Samarium has been detected on MASCARA–4b, a planet far beyond our solar system. Astronomers don't know why the planet has so much samarium.

Europium

Europium is named after Europe. It is the most reactive of the lanthanides, and it's fluorescent, with different ions glowing red and blue.

Doping

Europium's special role is in doping—small amounts are added to a material to change its properties. It makes phosphors in TV screens and fluorescent light bulbs glow more brightly. A europium-yttrium compound produces red on old cathode ray tube (CRT) television screens.

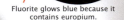
Fluorite glows blue because it contains europium.

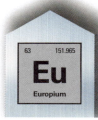

Atomic number: 63
Melting point: 822 °C (1,512 °F)
Boiling point: 1,529 °C (2,784 °F)
Earth crust: 2 ppm
Year of discovery: 1901
Group: N/A
Category: lanthanide

Gadolinium

Gadolinium makes useful alloys for magnets, electronic components, and data storage disks. It's also used as a neutron absorber in nuclear reactors.

Gadolinium is used to make the image clearer in magnetic resonance imaging (MRI) for diagnosing cancer.

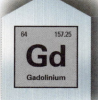

Atomic number: 64
Melting point: 1,313 °C (2,395 °F)
Boiling point: 3,273 °C (5,923 °F)
Earth crust: 8 ppm
Year of discovery: 1880
Group: N/A
Category: lanthanide

Magnetic Fridges

Gadolinium heats up in the presence of a magnetic field, so it's used in the cooling system of magnetic fridges. This new method of cooling fridges first became available commercially in 2016.

DID YOU KNOW? The amount and oxidation state of europium in Moon rock samples suggests that the Moon was formed from different cosmic material than the Earth.

Terbium

Terbium, like erbium (number 68), ytterbium (number 70), and yttrium (number 39), was first discovered in ore from a mine in Ytterby. This Swedish village gave its name to all four elements.

Terbium is a doping agent in semiconductors and was used in the production of the first rewritable compact discs. It's also used in lasers and X-rays.

Light and Sound

Terbium is luminescent, and some compounds are used in fiber optic sensors where they glow when stressed by forces. An alloy of terbium, iron, and dysprosium changes shape in a magnetic field. It enhances sound and can even turn a windowpane into a loudspeaker.

As a phosphor, terbium gives the yellow to fluorescent lamps and green to TV screens.

With europium and thulium, terbium is one of the three elements used in security codes in paper currency.

65 **158.92534**
Tb
Terbium

Atomic number: 65
Melting point: 1,359 °C (2,478 °F)
Boiling point: 3,230 °C (5,846 °F)
Earth crust: 1 ppm
Year of discovery: 1843
Group: N/A
Category: lanthanide

Dysprosium to Lutetium

Like others in the series, these six lanthanides are silvery metals. They have similar properties and specialized uses. Erbium is used in fiber optic cables, thulium reveals fake money, holmium and dysprosium are used in nuclear reactors, and ytterbium could one day make more accurate atomic clocks than cesium.

Erbium compounds give the hue to pink glass sculptures by Dale Chihuly.

Dy — Dysprosium — 66 — 162.50
Atomic number: 66
Melting point: 1,412 °C (2,574 °F)
Boiling point: 2,567 °C (4,653 °F)
Earth crust: trace amount
Year of discovery: 1886
Group: N/A
Category: lanthanide

Er — Erbium — 68 — 167.26
Atomic number: 68
Melting point: 1,529 °C (2,784 °F)
Boiling point: 2,868 °C (5,194 °F)
Earth crust: trace amount
Year of discovery: 1843
Group: N/A
Category: lanthanide

Ho — Holmium — 67 — 164.9303
Atomic number: 67
Melting point: 1,472 °C (2,682 °F)
Boiling point: 2,700 °C (4,892 °F)
Earth crust: trace amount
Year of discovery: 1878
Group: N/A
Category: lanthanide

DID YOU KNOW? In 1874, Robert Bunsen had to restart three years of analyzing the lanthanides, after his finished manuscript burned up in an accident.

Hard to Get

Paul-Émile Lecoq de Boisbaudran gave dysprosium a name meaning "hard to get," because it was difficult to extract from ores. Dysprosium could become even harder to get, as it's in demand for green energy uses like high-temperature magnets for electric cars and wind turbines—and it's starting to run out.

The lanthanides are expensive because they are hard to separate.

The heavier lanthanides are easily magnetized and are used in data storage devices like compact discs.

In 2017, IBM said it had created the world's smallest magnet and could store one bit of data on a single holmium atom.

Tm — Thulium
69   168.93421
Atomic number: 69
Melting point: 1,545 °C (2,813 °F)
Boiling point: 1,950 °C (3,542 °F)
Earth crust: trace amount
Year of discovery: 1879
Group: N/A
Category: lanthanide

Yb — Ytterbium
70   173.04
Atomic number: 70
Melting point: 824 °C (1,515 °F)
Boiling point: 1,196 °C (2,185 °F)
Earth crust: trace amount
Year of discovery: 1878
Group: N/A
Category: lanthanide

Lu — Lutetium
71   174.967
Atomic number: 71
Melting point: 1,663 °C (3,025 °F)
Boiling point: 3,402 °C (6,156 °F)
Earth crust: trace amount
Year of discovery: 1907
Group: N/A
Category: lanthanide

Hafnium to Osmium

Elements 72 to 76 are hard metals with extremely high melting points and corrosion-resistance. Their superstrong alloys and compounds are essential to the metal-working, mining, petroleum, and space industries.

Tungsten has the highest melting point of all metals. Tungsten and hafnium make excellent cutting, welding, and drilling tools.

Atomic number: 72
Melting point: 2,233 °C (4,051 °F)
Boiling point: 4,600 °C (8,312 °F)
Earth crust: 3 ppm
Year of discovery: 1923
Group: 4
Category: transition metal

Atomic number: 73
Melting point: 3,017 °C (5,463 °F)
Boiling point: 5,455 °C (9,851 °F)
Earth crust: 1 ppm
Year of discovery: 1802
Group: 5
Category: transition metal

Atomic number: 74
Melting point: 3,414 °C (6,177 °F)
Boiling point: 5,555 °C (10,031 °F)
Earth crust: 1 ppm
Year of discovery: 1783
Group: 6
Category: transition metal

DID YOU KNOW? A compound of hafnium, tungsten, and carbon melts at 4,125 °C (7,457 °F)—the highest melting point of any known compound.

Prosthetics and Pen Nibs

Tantalum doesn't cause an immune reaction, so it can be used in medicine to replace bone, connect nerves, and support muscles. Rhenium is very rare, but its alloys are used in oven filaments and X-ray machines. Osmium is the densest of all the elements. It's used in alloys for high-quality pen nibs. Rhenium, osmium, and hafnium catalysts are all used in the chemicals industry.

The engine rocket thruster nozzles of some space vehicles are a temperature-resistant superalloy of 10 percent hafnium, with niobium and titanium.

More Uses

Superstrong alloys of hafnium, tantalum, and rhenium are also used in aircraft and turbine blades. Hafnium rods also control the rate of the reaction in nuclear reactors and nuclear-powered submarines.

Re — Rhenium
75 186.207

Atomic number: 75
Melting point: 3,185 °C (5,765 °F)
Boiling point: 5,590 °C (10,094 °F)
Earth crust: trace amount
Year of discovery: 1925
Group: 7
Category: transition metal

Os — Osmium
76 190.23

Atomic number: 76
Melting point: 3,033 °C (5,491 °F)
Boiling point: 5,008 °C (9,046 °F)
Earth crust: trace amount
Year of discovery: 1803
Group: 8
Category: transition metal

Iridium

Iridium is a hard, silvery-white metal with a very high density and melting point. It's almost as unreactive as gold and is the most corrosion-resistant material. It's used in compasses and spark plugs.

Space Element

Iridium is one of the rarest elements. Deposits are found around the world, and probably arrived on asteroids. It's been back to space as a container for plutonium fuel on long-range probes and as a coating for telescope mirrors. Iridium is the next most dense element, after osmium. About 3 tonnes (3.3 tons) per year is produced as a byproduct of nickel refining.

Iridium, which makes colored salts, is named after Iris, the Greek goddess of rainbows. Iridescence—as in the shifting hues of insects' wings—also comes from Iris.

Until 2019, the mass of a cylinder of platinum–iridium alloy in a vault in France defined the kilogram weight. It's now defined mathematically.

77   192.217
Ir
Iridium

Atomic number: 77
Melting point: 2,446 °C (4,435 °F)
Boiling point: 4,428 °C (8,002 °F)
Earth crust: trace amount
Year of discovery: 1803
Group: 9
Category: transition metal

DID YOU KNOW? Smithson Tennant first separated osmium and iridium in 1804. He named iridium after beautiful rainbows and osmium after the Greek word for smell.

Platinum

More precious than silver, platinum is used in jewelry, vehicles, electronics, optical fibers, turbine blades, and medicine.

Precious Nuisance

Platinum was a nuisance to 16th-century gold miners because it was difficult to separate from gold. It became a precious metal in the 18th century when Antoine Lavoisier managed to make a furnace hot enough to melt and purify it. Its compound, cisplatin, is an important chemotherapy drug for treating cancer. Platinum catalysts are used in the chemicals and plastics industries and in fuel cells.

Around half of platinum demand is for catalytic converters, which reduce harmful emissions from vehicle engines.

Platinum can be used to coat dental implants, protecting them from corrosion (as shown in this model).

Platinum and iridium, along with palladium, rhodium, rutherium, and osmium, are the Platinum Group Metals (PGMs).

78   195.084
Pt
Platinum

Atomic number: 78
Melting point: 1,768 °C (3,215 °F)
Boiling point: 3,825 °C (6,917 °F)
Earth crust: trace amount
Year of discovery: 1735
Group: 10
Category: transition metal

Gold

Gold is a soft yellow metal. It's unreactive. That means it doesn't form minerals, and—like copper and silver (also in Group 11)—it's found naturally as nuggets. These three metals were the first elements people knew and used, but gold is the most prized.

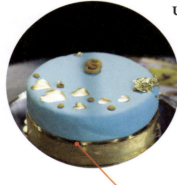

Food can be decorated with gold. It's safe to eat because it doesn't react with the body.

Uses for Gold

Gold is easily worked into objects (malleable) and pulled into wires (ductile). A thin layer of gold can be added to metal objects by electroplating, which is useful for gears in watches and electrical connections and circuits. Tiny gold nanoparticles (a nanometer is a billionth of a meter) are used as catalysts to make PVA glue. A gold compound is used to treat arthritis.

Alchemy Then and Now

Alchemists—early scientists—tried to turn ordinary metals like lead into gold, which they saw as the purest element. We now know we could, in theory, turn other atoms into gold by smashing particles together to change the nuclear structure. Sadly, any gold produced would be radioactive and too expensive to be useful.

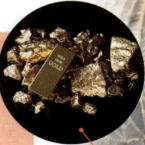

Most of the gold we use has been recycled many times. Only around 3,000 tonnes (3,307 tons) was mined in 2022.

DID YOU KNOW? The largest gold nugget ever found was 61 cm (24 in) long and weighed 71 kg (157 lb)—as much as a person!

The James Webb Space Telescope's 6.5 m (21 ft)–wide reflector is made of 18 gold-plated mirrors. The gold helps reflect as much light as possible.

Gold was being mined by the ancient Egyptians in 2000 BCE. Older graves from Ur (modern Iraq) have been found containing gold objects.

Gold has been used in coins and jewelry for thousands of years.

Egyptian king Tutankhamun had three coffins. One was solid gold and weighed 110 kg (243 lb).

79	196.967

Au
Gold

Atomic number: 79
Melting point: 1,064 °C (1,948 °F)
Boiling point: 2,836 °C (5,137 °F)
Earth crust: trace amount
Year of discovery: prehistory
Group: 11
Category: transition metal

Mercury

Your grandparents may have rolled liquid "beads" of mercury around in their hands at school. Perhaps they also have mercury amalgam fillings in their teeth. But mercury is much less used now that we know its dangers.

Highly Poisonous

Tiny amounts of mercury are in all living things, so during our lives we might safely take in 0.3 grams (0.01 oz). Higher doses are toxic. A compound called methylmercury is very dangerous if it accumulates in the environment and the food chain. It's also dangerous to breathe in, damaging the nerves and brain. Hat makers in the 18th and 19th centuries became seriously ill because they used mercury.

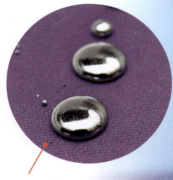

Mercury pours like a liquid, but it's so heavy that an iron nail will float on top.

Ancient Chinese objects were carved from cinnabar (mercury sulfide). Vermilion, a red pigment first used in 30,000-year-old cave paintings, is also cinnabar.

Applications

Mercury mixes with other metals to make mercury alloys, or amalgams. It amalgamates well with gold, so it can help extract gold from deposits. It has been used to produce chlorine, and in batteries and fluorescent lights. These applications are being phased out, but it is still used as a catalyst in the chemical industry, and in electrical devices.

DID YOU KNOW? Two tablespoons of mercury weigh about 545 grams (1 lb), about the same as 500 jelly beans.

Mercury is named after the planet Mercury, but its older name is "quicksilver." The chemical symbol Hg comes from the Greek "hydrargyrum," meaning liquid silver.

Mercury is a heavy, silvery liquid—the only metal that's liquid at room temperature.

People have been fascinated by mercury for over 3,000 years, even drinking it in the hope it would help them live forever.

Mercury has been widely used in scientific instruments, such as thermometers and barometers.

Atomic number: 80
Melting point: −39 °C (−38 °F)
Boiling point: 357 °C (674 °F)
Earth crust: trace amount
Year of discovery: prehistory
Group: 12
Category: transition metal

80 200.592
Hg
Mercury

Thallium

Thallium makes compounds that dissolve easily have no smell or taste and are highly toxic. In the past, it has been used as a rat killer—and murder weapon.

Jumble of Properties

Thallium is a soft, conductive metal with a low melting point, like lead; it is photosensitive, like silver; and it poisons by damaging the nervous system, like mercury. Thallium sulfide is useful in photoelectric cells because its conductivity changes in infrared light. Thallium also makes glass with a low melting point for electronics.

Chemist Jean-Baptiste Dumas called thallium the "duck-billed platypus of the metals." Just as the platypus is similar to an otter, a beaver, and a duck, so thallium is similar to several other elements.

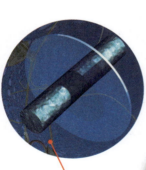

This image represents both the meaning of the word thallium—"green shoot"—and the use of the toxic metal in optical lenses.

Atomic number: 81
Melting point: 304 °C (579 °F)
Boiling point: 1,473 °C (2,683 °F)
Earth crust: 1 ppm
Year of discovery: 1861
Group: 13
Category: post-transition metal

Lead

Soft, gray, malleable, and unreactive, lead has been used in building materials for thousands of years. Its chemical symbol—and the word for plumbers—comes from its Latin name, "plumbum."

Stained-glass windows have pieces of lead holding the panels in place.

Heavyweight

Lead makes bendable pipes and waterproofing seals for roofs. It was used in paints and gasoline until the second half of the 20th century. But lead is toxic and builds up in the body, so many uses have been phased out. It's still used in car batteries, pigments, solders, crystal glass, and lead weights.

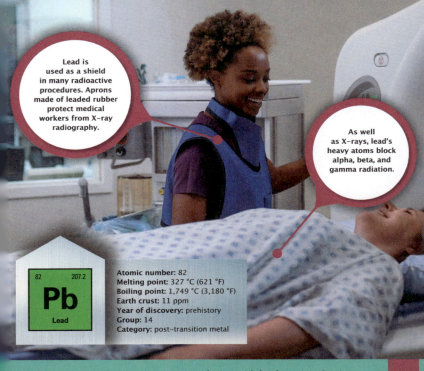

Lead is used as a shield in many radioactive procedures. Aprons made of leaded rubber protect medical workers from X-ray radiography.

As well as X-rays, lead's heavy atoms block alpha, beta, and gamma radiation.

Pb — 82 — 207.2 — Lead

Atomic number: 82
Melting point: 327 °C (621 °F)
Boiling point: 1,749 °C (3,180 °F)
Earth crust: 11 ppm
Year of discovery: prehistory
Group: 14
Category: post-transition metal

DID YOU KNOW? The Romans sweetened wine with lead acetate. Putting lead in your wine is a bad idea—perhaps it sped up the fall of the Roman Empire!

Bismuth

Elements after lead are all radioactive. But bismuth's half-life—over a billion times longer than the age of the Universe—is so long, it's hardly radioactive at all.

Melted bismuth cools to make angular, rainbow-effect crystals.

Very Safe

Bismuth is a heavy, brittle, pinkish-silver metal. It's used in catalysts and low-melting-point alloys with tin or cadmium, and for fire extinguishers, electrical fuses, and solders. Bismuth oxide is safely used in cosmetics, and bismuth carbonate is an indigestion medicine.

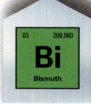

83 208.980
Bi
Bismuth

Atomic number: 83
Melting point: 271 °C (521 °F)
Boiling point: 1,564 °C (2,847 °F)
Earth crust: trace amount
Year of discovery: around 1500
Group: 15
Category: post-transition metal

Polonium

Mendeleev predicted the existence of an element after bismuth. After a long search, Marie and Pierre Curie finally found polonium in uranium ore.

The Soviet "Luna" program explored the Moon's surface with rovers, powered by the heat from polonium radioactivity.

84 (209)
Po
Polonium

Atomic number: 84
Melting point: 254 °C (489 °F)
Boiling point: 962 °C (1,764 °F)
Earth crust: trace amount
Year of discovery: 1898
Group: 16
Category: metalloid

High Radioactivity

Sadly, Marie Curie died because of her work with radioactive elements. Polonium is used in antistatic devices, but it has few other uses.

Astatine

Astatine may be the rarest element in nature, but it decays too quickly to know for sure. Tiny amounts have been produced. It may one day be useful in radiotherapy.

A mineral sample of autunite might contain a few astatine atoms.

Little Studied

Astatine is made by bombarding bismuth with neutrons. It's little understood because it's so radioactive, but it's chemically similar to iodine and the other halogens.

Atomic number: 85
Melting point: 300 °C (572 °F)
Boiling point: 350 °C (662 °F)
Earth crust: trace amount
Year of discovery: 1940
Group: 17
Category: halogen

Radon

Period 6 ends with radon, the heaviest gas known. It's unreactive, colorless, and odorless—but dangerously radioactive. Its half-life is three days.

In 1984, a nuclear power plant worker learned he had radon in his basement, when he set off radiation alarms as he went into work.

Household Hazard

Radon is produced by the natural decay of radium and is found in igneous rocks like granite. In buildings made of granite or built on granite-rich soils, the heavy gas can accumulate in unventilated spaces.

Atomic number: 86
Melting point: −71 °C (−96 °F)
Boiling point: −62 °C (−79 °F)
Earth crust: trace amount
Year of discovery: 1900
Group: 18
Category: noble gas

DID YOU KNOW? There's probably less than 50 mg (0.002 ounces) of astatine in the Earth's crust.

Chapter 6: Period 7: Francium to Oganesson

Francium

Period 7 elements are radioactive—they decay by emitting radiation. They are mostly very rare. The first is francium in Group 1. Mendeleev had predicted an unknown element that behaved like cesium, and 70 years later, Marguerite Perey found francium from the radioactive decay of actinium.

Intensely Radioactive

Francium's position on the Periodic Table tells us it's an extremely reactive alkali metal. The melting points of the alkali metals get lower as you go down the Group, so francium would be liquid at room temperature—if it wasn't too radioactive to hang around! It has a half-life of 22 minutes—the time for half of it to decay into radium.

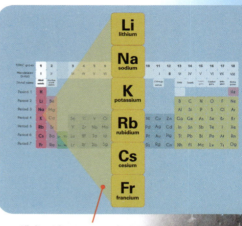

Alkali metals get more reactive as you go down the Group. Francium should be the most reactive—but it's so heavy that it behaves oddly. It's slightly less reactive than cesium.

This artistic representation of francium shows a winged helmet, traditionally used to represent the Celts. Francium, like gallium, is named after France—home of the ancient Celts.

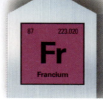

Atomic number: 87
Melting point: 21 °C (70 °F)
Boiling point: 650 °C (1,202 °F)
Earth crust: trace amount
Year of discovery: 1939
Group: 1
Category: alkali metal

DID YOU KNOW? Marguerite Perey and Marie Curie both died of cancer caused by their radioactivity research. Marie Curie's notebooks are still radioactive today.

Radium

Radium is the most radioactive natural element. If you could hold it, the soft silvery metal would feel warm and crackle on your skin. Like other Group 2 metals, it would tarnish in air.

Radium was once used in luminous paints on clocks. Tragically, many workers who painted the dials died.

Fascinating Glow

When Pierre and Marie Curie discovered radium in uranium ore, people were fascinated by its eerie blue glow. They even used it as a hair restorer! Radium has few uses now that its dangers are known, but it's still used to treat bone cancer.

Radium emits alpha, beta, and gamma particles. People working with radium must be protected with lead shielding.

Alpha particles can't penetrate skin; beta particles (electrons) are stopped by aluminum; and gamma rays are stopped by lead.

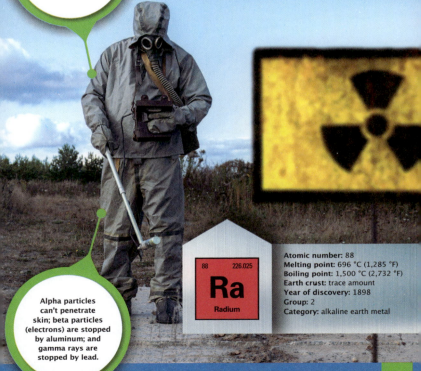

88	226.025
Ra	
Radium	

Atomic number: 88
Melting point: 696 °C (1,285 °F)
Boiling point: 1,500 °C (2,732 °F)
Earth crust: trace amount
Year of discovery: 1898
Group: 2
Category: alkaline earth metal

Actinium

Element numbers 89 to 103 are the actinides, named after the first one—actinium. The series of 15 highly radioactive, silvery metals was added to the Periodic Table in 1945.

Like uranium, polonium, and radium, actinium was first isolated from pitchblende (uranium ore). One tonne (0.9 tons) of rock contains around 150 mg (0.005 oz) of actinium.

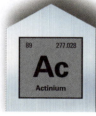

Atomic number: 89
Melting point: 1,050 °C (1,922 °F)
Boiling point: 3,200 °C (5,792 °F)
Earth crust: trace amount
Year of discovery: 1899
Group: 3
Category: actinide

Isotopes

Actinium has 36 isotopes. Actinium-227 has a half-life of 22 years and changes into thorium-227. Actinium-225 has a half-life of 10 days and eventually decays into bismuth-213, which is used to treat cancer.

Thorium

Jöns Jakob Berzelius, who had already discovered three elements, extracted thorium in 1829 and named it after Thor, god of war. It is weakly radioactive with a half-life of 14 billion years.

Abundant

Thorium is abundant—Earth's crust has three times more thorium than uranium. Thorium oxide has the highest melting point of any oxide—3,300 °C (5,972 °F). It's used in crucibles for high-temperature research.

Atomic number: 90
Melting point: 1,750 °C (3,182 °F)
Boiling point: 4,785 °C (8,645 °F)
Earth crust: 6 ppm
Year of discovery: 1829
Group: N/A
Category: actinide

DID YOU KNOW? Actinium is 150 times more radioactive than radium. It's considered even more dangerous than plutonium.

Protactinium

Protactinium is highly radioactive and decays to form actinium. The Greek word "protos" means first—protactinium's name means "origin of actinium."

Single Sample

Protactinium is made by uranium decay. Tiny amounts exist in uranium ores, but research laboratories have been supplied from a 125-g (4.4-oz) sample, produced in 1961 from 54 tonnes (60 tons) of radioactive waste.

Protactinium emits alpha particles to become actinium. The Japanese monogram "ichi" reflects the "first" in protactinium's name.

Scientists study ocean movements from the last ice age by measuring the ratio of protactinium-231 and thorium-230 in the sea floor.

Ice ages happen over thousands of years. Protactinium helps scientists investigate how current global warming might affect the ice age cycle.

91 231.03588
Pa
Protactinium

Atomic number: 91
Melting point: 1,572 °C (2,862 °F)
Boiling point: 4,000 °C (7,232 °F)
Earth crust: trace amount
Year of discovery: 1913
Group: N/A
Category: actinide

Uranium

Uranium is most important for generating electricity in nuclear power stations. It's also used to make isotopes of other elements. The alpha particles it emits can't get through skin but are harmful if they enter the body. Uranium is also dangerously chemically toxic if eaten.

Nuclear Fuel

Uranium is found in ores like pitchblende. Natural uranium is mostly uranium-238, with 1 percent uranium-235. Processing enriches (increases) the U-235. U-235 is used as fuel in nuclear power plants because it's fissionable—its nuclei can split in a chain reaction. World production of uranium is around 41,000 tonnes (45,195 tons) per year.

Uranium ore is purified to make "yellow-cake"—uranium oxide—which is processed to make uranium fuel.

Huge amounts of energy are released by nuclear fission. Nuclear power plants use the energy to make electricity.

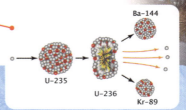

Nuclear Fission

The mass number of uranium-235 is 235 because one nucleus has 92 protons plus 143 neutrons. When a uranium-235 nucleus absorbs a neutron, it becomes uranium-236. But the nucleus can't hold all those neutrons, and it splits in two. This fission produces smaller elements and free neutrons. Free neutrons bombard more uranium-235 nuclei, which also split in a chain reaction.

DID YOU KNOW? In theory, 1 kg (2.2 lb) of uranium-235 can produce as much energy as 1,500,000 kg (1,653 tons) of coal.

112

Neptunium

The elements after uranium, from number 93 to number 118, are the transuranium elements. Apart from neptunium and americium, they aren't found in nature. Scientists synthesize them by making existing atoms absorb extra particles.

Development of The Bomb

Neptunium and plutonium were created in 1940 by smashing neutrons into uranium-238. A uranium-238 nucleus that absorbed a neutron eventually decayed into plutonium-239— the basis of the atomic bombs developed during World War II.

Making Neptunium

The neutron in a uranium atom can break up into a proton and an electron. The electron escapes as beta radiation. The nucleus is left with one more proton—so uranium becomes neptunium.

Atomic number: 93
Melting point: 644 °C (1,191 °F)
Boiling point: 3,902 °C (7,056 °F)
Earth crust: trace amount
Year of discovery: 1940
Group: N/A
Category: actinide

Plutonium

Plutonium is very toxic because of its radioactivity. It's been used in the most terrifying weapons humans have invented, so it has a terrible reputation. But it's not all bad.

The Good Side

Plutonium is an energy source in space, and it's been used in heart pacemakers. Interestingly, it forms six different allotropes at different temperatures, and it has unusual magnetic properties and oxidation states.

Plutonium supplied power in the New Horizons Space Probe's generator.

Atomic number: 94
Melting point: 640 °C (1,184 °F)
Boiling point: 3,228 °C (5,842 °F)
Earth crust: N/A
Year of discovery: 1940
Group: N/A
Category: actinide

Americium

Americium is 60 times more expensive than gold. It's only used in jobs where tiny amounts are needed, such as in smoke alarms and as a source of alpha and gamma radiation for medical and industrial uses.

> Alpha particles from americium ionize the air in smoke detectors, letting an electric current flow. Smoke absorbs the particles and stops the current, so the alarm rings.

The Light Side of Manhattan

Glenn T. Seaborg and colleagues working on the Manhattan Project made americium and curium in 1944. Instead of first announcing it at a science conference, Seaborg let the news slip on a children's radio show! Before choosing the names americium and curium, the scientists jokingly called the new elements delirium and pandemonium.

> A smoke alarm contains less than a millionth of a gram of americium-241 oxide. It decays into neptunium-237 very slowly. Its half-life is 432 years.

Americium sits under europium on the Periodic Table, so its US discoverers named it after their own continent.

Atomic number: 95
Melting point: 1,176 °C (2,149 °F)
Boiling point: 2,011 °C (3,652 °F)
Earth crust: trace amount
Year of discovery: 1944
Group: N/A
Category: actinide

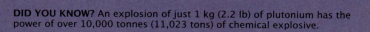

DID YOU KNOW? An explosion of just 1 kg (2.2 lb) of plutonium has the power of over 10,000 tonnes (11,023 tons) of chemical explosive.

115

Curium to Mendelevium

Four of these six synthetic elements are named in honor of pioneering scientists: Pierre and Marie Curie, Albert Einstein, Enrico Fermi, and Dmitri Mendeleev. The remaining two are named after where they were first made—Berkeley, California.

Curium is used as space fuel and in alpha particle X-ray spectrometers (APXS)—used by planetary rovers to study soil and rocks.

Atomic number: 96
Melting point: 1,345 °C (2,543 °F)
Boiling point: unknown
Earth crust: N/A
Year of discovery: 1944
Group: N/A
Category: actinide

Atomic number: 97
Melting point: 986 °C (1,807 °F)
Boiling point: unknown
Earth crust: N/A
Year of discovery: 1949
Group: N/A
Category: actinide

Atomic number: 98
Melting point: 900 °C (1,652 °F)
Boiling point: unknown
Earth crust: N/A
Year of discovery: 1950
Group: N/A
Category: actinide

Tiny Amounts

Californium emits a flow of neutrons that can be used to identify metal ores, explore oil wells, and detect metal fatigue in aircraft. Berkelium, einsteinium, fermium, and mendelevium are only used in research. They're made in tiny amounts and their isotopes decay quickly. It took nine years to produce enough berkelium to be visible.

> A particle accelerator works by whirling particles around and then throwing them at target atoms at speed, like a shot-putter.

Atomic number: 99
Melting point: 860 °C (1,580 °F)
Boiling point: unknown
Earth crust: N/A
Year of discovery: 1952
Group: N/A
Category: actinide

> Modern versions of the cyclotron are used in radiotherapy—targeting and killing cancer cells with beams of protons or other particles.

Atomic number: 100
Melting point: 1,527 °C (2,781 °F)
Boiling point: unknown
Earth crust: N/A
Year of discovery: 1953
Group: N/A
Category: actinide

> Berkeley scientists in the 1940s and '50s used an early particle accelerator called a cyclotron to bombard atoms and make new elements.

Atomic number: 101
Melting point: 827 °C (1,521 °F)
Boiling point: unknown
Earth crust: N/A
Year of discovery: 1955
Group: N/A
Category: actinide

DID YOU KNOW? Just 17 atoms of mendelevium were produced when Berkeley scientists first made it by bombarding einsteinium in the cyclotron, in 1955.

Nobelium

It's hard to prove that you've made a few atoms when they are too small to see and so heavy that they quickly fall apart. Disputes between research teams can be long and bitter. The International Union of Pure and Applied Chemists (IUPAC) decides who discovered an element first and who has the right to name it.

Argument

Nobelium's discovery caused a lot of argument. Between 1956 and 1963, research teams in Russia, the USA, and the Nobel Institute of Physics in Sweden all joined the race to make isotopes of element 102. After years of argument, IUPAC declared the Russians the winners.

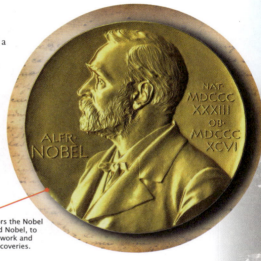

Nobelium's name honors the Nobel Prize, set up by Alfred Nobel, to reward outstanding work and groundbreaking discoveries.

The Russian team wanted to call the element joliotium, after Irène Joliot–Curie, but it had been called nobelium for so long, the name stuck.

Atomic number: 102
Melting point: 827 °C (1,521 °F)
Boiling point: unknown
Earth crust: N/A
Year of discovery: 1963
Group: N/A
Category: actinide

DID YOU KNOW? Scientists still can't agree whether nobelium should be pronounced nobel–ium or nobeelium (to rhyme with helium).

Lawrencium

Lawrencium is another very heavy radioactive metal. Big, synthetic elements like this can't hold together. They decay quickly, and they are highly radioactive. They are all very difficult to study!

More Argument

The discovery of lawrencium also caused arguments between teams at the Lawrence Berkeley Laboratory, USA, who attempted to make isotopes in 1958, 1960, and 1961, and the Joint Institute for Nuclear Research in Russia, who made it from americium in 1965. IUPAC awarded the discovery to the Lawrence team.

> The Lawrence Berkeley National Laboratory was founded by Nobel Prize winner Ernest O. Lawrence. The laboratory and lawrencium are both named after him.

> In the first cyclotron, particles accelerated in an electromagnetic field in an object just 11 cm (4 in) across.

> Ernest Lawrence invented the cyclotron in 1930. The modern Large Hadron Collider is a much bigger version of the cyclotron.

Atomic number: 103
Melting point: 1,627 °C (2,961 °F)
Boiling point: unknown
Earth crust: N/A
Year of discovery: 1961
Group: N/A
Category: actinide

Rutherfordium

In the 1960s and '70s, scientists in the USA, Russia, and other countries raced to create the heaviest elements of Period 7. They made rutherfordium, dubnium, and seaborgium, producing just a few atoms of each.

Rutherford Honored

In 1992, the world authority, IUPAC, credited the discovery of rutherfordium to scientists in both Russia and the USA. They named the element after Ernest Rutherford, who discovered atomic structure and pioneered the study of radioactivity.

> Rutherford invented the term "half-life" for the time it takes for half the atoms in a radioactive sample to decay into atoms of a different element.

> "Halflife," a 2015 art installation in London, was inspired by the term for the decay period of radioactive elements.

> Rutherfordium's half-life is minutes, yet scientists have managed to show that it reacts like zirconium and hafnium in Group 4.

104 (267)
Rf
Rutherfordium

Atomic number: 104
Melting point: unknown
Boiling point: unknown
Earth crust: N/A
Year of discovery: 1964
Group: 4
Category: transuranium

Dubnium

The elements heavier than fermium caused such arguments over their discovery that, in 1986, IUPAC and the equivalent authority for physics—IUPAP—set up the Transfermium Working Group to resolve the issues.

Dubnium was named after the Russian town Dubna.

Long-running Dispute

Scientists claiming to have created dubnium argued for nearly 30 years. Eventually, joint credit was given to scientists at Joint Institute for Nuclear Research in Dubna, Russia, and in Berkeley, USA.

Atomic number: 105
Melting point: unknown
Boiling point: unknown
Earth crust: N/A
Year of discovery: 1968–70
Group: 5
Category: transuranium

Seaborgium

Superheavy elements are made by bombarding heavy nuclei with lighter nuclei so they fuse. Target element californium-249 was bombarded with carbon to make rutherfordium, with nitrogen to make dubnium, and with oxygen to make seaborgium.

Atomic Chemistry

Glenn T. Seaborg discovered several transuranium elements. He developed ways to extract individual atoms as they were created, so their chemical reactions could be studied before they decayed.

Seaborg was honored during his own lifetime by the naming of seaborgium.

Atomic number: 106
Melting point: unknown
Boiling point: unknown
Earth crust: N/A
Year of discovery: 1974
Group: 6
Category: transuranium

DID YOU KNOW? One atom per hour of seaborgium–263 was produced by scientists bombarding californium with oxygen. Its half-life is 0.8 seconds.

Bohrium to Copernicium

Just a few atoms of these six superheavy elements have been produced for research. Their discovery is credited to the German nuclear research institute (GSI). Hassium and Darmstadtium are named after GSI's facility in Darmstadt, Hesse.

Bohrium is named after Neils Bohr, who worked with Ernest Rutherford to refine Rutherford's model of atomic structure.

1807 model · 1897 model · 1911: Rutherford's model · 1913: Bohr's model

Atomic number: 107
Melting point: unknown
Boiling point: unknown
Earth crust: N/A
Year of discovery: 1981
Group: 7
Category: transuranium

Atomic number: 108
Melting point: unknown
Boiling point: unknown
Earth crust: N/A
Year of discovery: 1984
Group: 8
Category: transuranium

Atomic number: 109
Melting point: unknown
Boiling point: unknown
Earth crust: N/A
Year of discovery: 1982
Group: 9
Category: transuranium

DID YOU KNOW? In 1982, GSI bombarded bismuth with iron for a week, creating just one atom of meitnerium. It decayed in 5 milliseconds.

Predictable Behavior

The GSI particle accelerator smashes nuclei together to make heavier elements. They quickly decay into smaller, stable atoms—yet experiments have been done to show that even these superheavy atoms have chemical properties that fit with their positions on the Periodic Table.

> Electromagnets blast the ions at up to one-fifth the speed of light. They need enough energy for colliding nuclei to fuse, but not so much that they fall apart.

> GSI's universal linear accelerator (UNILAC) shoots ions at target nuclei at the end of a 120-m (394-ft) tube.

> A few nuclei fuse and are collected and identified. Just one second gives scientists enough time to do chemical tests.

Atomic number: 110
Melting point: unknown
Boiling point: unknown
Earth crust: N/A
Year of discovery: 1994
Group: 10
Category: transuranium

Atomic number: 111
Melting point: unknown
Boiling point: unknown
Earth crust: N/A
Year of discovery: 1994
Group: 11
Category: transuranium

Atomic number: 112
Melting point: unknown
Boiling point: unknown
Earth crust: N/A
Year of discovery: 1996
Group: 12
Category: transuranium

Nihonium to Oganesson

Period 7 of the Periodic Table was completed in 2016, when nihonium, moscovium, tennessine, and oganesson were added. Their new names replaced temporary placeholder names. These old names were their atomic numbers in Latin—so moscovium was ununpentium—meaning one-one-five.

Renowned nuclear physicist Yuri Oganessian was honored in his lifetime with oganesson.

Nh — Nihonium (113, (284))
Atomic number: 113
Melting point: unknown
Boiling point: unknown
Earth crust: N/A
Year of discovery: 2004
Group: 13
Category: transuranium

Fl — Flerovium (114, (289))
Atomic number: 114
Melting point: unknown
Boiling point: unknown
Earth crust: N/A
Year of discovery: 1999
Group: 14
Category: transuranium

Mc — Moscovium (115, (288))
Atomic number: 115
Melting point: unknown
Boiling point: unknown
Earth crust: N/A
Year of discovery: 2010
Group: 15
Category: transuranium

Lv — Livermorium (116, (292))
Atomic number: 116
Melting point: unknown
Boiling point: unknown
Earth crust: N/A
Year of discovery: 2000
Group: 16
Category: transuranium

Cooperative Research

The superheavy elements were discovered after years of painstaking experiments by a few specialized laboratories. By the end of the 20th century, research teams were joining forces. Livermorium reflects cooperation—it was made in Russia by nuclear fusion of curium from the USA, and named after the Lawrence Livermore National Laboratory (LLNL) in California.

> Nuclear fusion might in future provide limitless clean energy—replacing or supplementing wind turbines and helping humanity toward environmental sustainability.

> Even heavier superheavy elements could be waiting to be discovered. It's possible they might be less fragile, offering more possibilities for research.

Atomic number: 117
Melting point: unknown
Boiling point: unknown
Earth crust: N/A
Year of discovery: 2010
Group: 17
Category: transuranium

Atomic number: 118
Melting point: unknown
Boiling point: unknown
Earth crust: N/A
Year of discovery: 2006
Group: 18
Category: transuranium

DID YOU KNOW? A weird rule of the Periodic Table is that elements with even-numbered atomic numbers are more naturally abundant than those with odd numbers.

Glossary

ABUNDANT
Plentiful, available in large quantities.

ACID
A chemical with a value lower than 7 on the pH scale.

ALCHEMIST
An early scientist who hoped to change substances such as ordinary metals into gold.

ALKALI
A chemical with a value higher than 7 on the pH scale.

ALLOTROPE
A form of an element with different arrangements of atoms.

ALLOY
A mixture of a metal with a different element, often another metal.

ANODIZE
To add a layer of oxide on a metal.

ATOM
The smallest unit of a chemical element.

ATOMIC NUMBER
The number of protons in an atom. An element's atomic number decides its position on the Periodic Table.

BIG BANG
The explosive beginning of the Universe, nearly 14 billion years ago.

CHEMICAL BOND
A force that joins atoms together, made by sharing, losing, or gaining electrons.

CHEMICAL REACTION
A process in which atoms are rearranged, changing one or more substances into different substances.

CHLOROPHYLL
A green pigment in plants that absorbs energy from sunlight for photosynthesis.

CLIMATE CHANGE
A gradual change in Earth's average global temperature.

COMPOUND
A pure chemical made from the atoms of more than one element.

CONDUCTOR
A material that lets heat or electricity pass through it.

CRYSTAL
A solid material in which the particles are joined together in a repeating pattern.

DECAY SERIES
The chain of elements made from decay of a radioactive isotope.

DENSITY
The space a substance takes up (its volume) in relation to the amount of matter in the substance (its mass).

DISSOLVE
When a solid is mixed with a liquid and it seems to disappear, it has dissolved.

DNA
A molecule that carries instructions for the structure and function of living things.

DOPING
To add a small amount of a substance to a material in order to improve it.

ELECTRON
A negatively charged particle found in an atom.

ELEMENT
A chemical made of a single type of atom. Elements are the simplest chemicals.

ENERGY SHELL
Also called electron shell or energy level; a cloud-like area around an atom's nucleus, where electrons move around.

FORMULA
Chemical symbols showing the number and type of atoms present in a molecule.

FOSSIL FUELS
Coal, crude oil, and natural gas. They are nonrenewable energy sources that add to climate change.

HALF-LIFE
The time it takes for half the nuclei in a radioactive sample to decay.

HYDROCARBON
A molecule containing only carbon and hydrogen atoms.

INSULATOR
A material that heat or electricity cannot pass through.

ION
An atom that carries an electric charge because it has lost or gained an electron. A cation is a positive ion, and an anion is a negative ion.

ISOTOPES
Forms of an element where the atoms have different numbers of neutrons.

MATERIAL
What a substance is made of, for example, ceramic or metal.

MATTER
What everything in the Universe is made of. All matter is made up of tiny particles called atoms.

METALLOID
An element that sometimes behaves like a metal; a semi-metal.

MINERAL
A naturally occurring inorganic solid with a defined chemical structure.

MOLECULE
A group of two or more atoms that are chemically bonded. The smallest unit of a pure substance that has the chemical properties of the substance.

NANOPARTICLE
A particle no more than 100 nanometers (0.0001 mm) long or wide.

NEUTRON
A particle found in the nucleus of an atom. Neutrons have no charge (neither positive nor negative).

NUCLEUS
The center of an atom. The plural is nuclei.

ORGANIC CHEMICALS
Carbon-based compounds. Living bodies are built from organic chemicals.

OXIDATION
A reaction in which a chemical gains oxygen atoms. The substance that gains oxygen is oxidized.

OXIDATION STATE
The number of electrons an atom has lost or gained in a reaction.

PHOTOSYNTHESIS
A process plants use to produce glucose and oxygen, using water, carbon dioxide, and energy from sunlight.

POLYMER
A very large, chain-like molecule made of repeated smaller molecules.

PPM
Parts per million; the number of atoms of an element in 1 million atoms of the Earth's crust.

PROTON
A positively charged particle found in the nucleus (center) of an atom.

RADIOACTIVE
A radioactive element decays and gives off radiation—small particles of energy.

REACTIVITY
How easily a substance reacts with other substances.

RESPIRATION
The process living things use to release energy from the breakdown of glucose.

SEMICONDUCTOR
A material that lets electricity flow through it under some conditions.

SOLUTION
What is created when a substance dissolves in a liquid.

STATES OF MATTER
Solid, liquid, or gas; matter takes a different state depending on how its molecules are arranged.

SUBATOMIC PARTICLES
Particles inside an atom, including electrons, protons, and neutrons.

SUPERCONDUCTOR
Material that lets electricity flow through with no resistance and no loss of energy.

SUPERFLUID
A fluid that flows without friction and with no loss of energy.

SYNTHETIC
Human-made, not naturally occurring.

TARNISH
When a metal reacts with oxygen in the air, it goes dull and tarnishes.

Index

actinides 7, 110–19
actinium (Ac) 110–13
allotropes 15, 32, 34, 44, 46, 66, 80, 82, 114
alloys 20, 31, 54, 55, 57–8, 60–2, 72, 74, 79–81, 88–90, 93, 96–8, 106
aluminum (Al) 30, 31, 42, 54, 60, 64
antimony (Te) 80, 82
argon (Ar) 17, 49, 69
arsenic (As) 21, 66, 82
atomic bonds 14–15, 17, 18, 35, 36, 47
atomic nucleus 12–13, 24
atomic number 4, 7, 12, 24–5
atomic structure 12–13, 122
atoms 4–8, 10–17, 24–5, 26, 28, 34, 73, 86, 117

barium (Ba) 87
berkelium (Bk) 116, 117
beryllium (Be) 31, 41
bismuth (Bi) 106, 110
boron (B) 32–3, 90

cadmium (Cd) 67, 78, 106, 113
cesium (Cs) 23, 38, 86, 94, 108
calcium (Ca) 9, 52–3
californium (Cf) 116–17, 121
carbon (C) 9, 14, 15, 19, 34–5, 43, 58–9
carbon dioxide (CO2) 9, 14, 34, 37, 40
catalysts 75, 82, 99, 102, 106
cerium (Ce) 89, 90
charge 12, 13, 14, 18, 56
chemical reactions 18
chlorine (Cl) 8, 14, 48, 102
chromium (Cr) 18, 31, 56, 59, 61
cobalt (Co) 58, 60
columns 6, 16
compounds 7, 8–9, 18, 20
conductors 19, 29, 31, 62, 72–3, 76, 80
copernicium (Cn) 123
copper (Cu) 18, 20, 31, 62–3, 67, 74, 77, 80
covalent bonds 14, 18
curium (Cm) 115, 116, 125

diatomic molecules 36
dysprosium (Dy) 93, 94–5

einsteinium (Es) 116, 117
electricity 15, 67, 112–13
electromagnets 29, 123
electrons 12–18, 24–6, 30, 38–40, 50, 56, 69, 81, 86, 114
elements 4, 6, 7, 8–9, 12, 16, 18, 20, 117
energy, sustainable 5, 67, 69, 74, 75, 125
energy shells 12–14, 16–17, 24–6, 28, 30, 39, 40, 50, 69, 81, 86

erbium (Er) 93, 94
europium (Eu) 92, 93

fermium (Fm) 117, 121
fluorine (F) 38, 48

gallium (Ga) 64, 67, 108
gases 10–11, 22
 see also specific gases
germanium (Ge) 65
gold (Au) 7–8, 13, 20–1, 54, 76, 79, 98–101, 115
Groups 4, 6, 16–17, 24

hafnium (Hf) 96–7, 120
half-life 91, 106–8, 110, 115, 120
halogens 16–17, 24, 38, 48, 68, 83, 107
helium (He) 9, 19, 28–9, 39
hydrocarbons 34, 95
hydrogen (H) 6–9, 18–19, 26–7, 34, 88

indium (In) 67, 79
iodine (I) 23, 83
ionic bonds 14, 15, 18
ions 14, 18, 40, 48, 50, 56–7, 61, 123
iridium (Ir) 75, 98, 99
iron (Fe) 58–9, 61, 90, 93
isotopes 7, 12, 23, 71, 88, 91, 110, 112, 117

krypton (Kr) 69, 84

lanthanides 6–7, 72, 88–95
lanthanum (La) 88, 90
lead (Pb) 16, 21, 56, 80–2, 105
limestone (calcium carbonate) 52–3, 58–9
lithium (Li) 7, 12, 17, 30, 41, 57, 61
livermorium (Lv) 124, 125

magnesium (Mg) 9, 41, 52, 57
magnets 29, 58, 60, 72–3, 80, 90–2, 95, 114, 123
manganese (Mn) 57
mass number 12
matter, states of 10–11
meitnerium (Mt) 25, 122
Mendeleev, Dmitri 5, 22–3, 64–5, 106, 108
mendelevium (Md) 117
mercury (Hg) 102–3
metalloids (semi-metals) 18, 19, 22, 32–3, 43, 65–6, 82, 106
metals 18–19, 20, 30–1, 60, 64
 alkali 7, 17, 40, 50–1, 70, 86, 108
 alkaline earth 16–17, 31, 41, 52–3, 71, 87, 109
 Platinum Group 75, 76, 99
 post-transition 6, 42, 64, 79–81, 104–6
 rare earth 54, 88
 transition 6, 18, 54–63, 72–8, 96–103
mixtures 8, 9
molecules 10, 14

neodymium (Nd) 90
neon (Ne) 17, 28, 39
neptunium (Np) 114, 115
neutrons 12, 16, 26, 28, 91, 107, 112–14, 117
nickel (Ni) 31, 58, 60, 61, 63, 74, 78, 98
niobium (Nb) 72, 97
nitrogen (N) 8, 36, 45, 73, 121
nobelium (No) 118
noble gases 17, 24, 39, 49, 69, 84–5, 107

non-metals 18–19, 22, 34–7, 38, 44–7, 67, 81
nuclear fission 25, 112–13
nuclear fusion 5, 27, 39, 69, 125

organesson (Og) 6, 124, 125
organic chemicals 19, 34
osmium (Os) 75, 97, 98, 99
oxidation states 18, 56, 93, 114
oxides 18, 21, 31, 54, 79, 88–9, 110, 112, 115
oxygen (O) 7–9, 12, 14, 18–19, 24–5, 28, 31, 34, 39, 42–3, 57, 86, 89, 121

palladium (Pd) 74, 75, 99
Periodic Table
 first 22–3
 reading the 24–5
 structure of the 16–17
Periods 4, 6, 16–17, 24
phosphorus (P) 7, 19, 36, 44–5
plasma 11
platinum (Pt) 74, 75, 98, 99
plutonium (Pu) 98, 110, 114
polonium (Po) 106, 110
potassium (K) 9, 50–1
protons 12–13, 16, 24, 26, 28, 112

radioactivity 13, 19, 25, 28, 50, 88, 91, 100, 105–21
radium (Ra) 109, 110
rhenium (Re) 96–7
rhodium (Rh) 74, 75, 99
rows 6, 16, 24
rubidium (Rb) 23, 70, 71
ruthenium (Ru) 74, 75, 99
rutherfordium (Rf) 120, 121

scandium (Sc) 54, 88
seaborgium (Sg) 120, 121
semiconductors 19, 28, 64–7, 78, 82, 93
silicon (Si) 18–19, 31, 42–3
silver (Ag) 76–7, 104
sodium (Na) 7–9, 14–16, 40–1, 48
sodium chloride (NaCl) 8, 14–15, 40, 48
solids 10–11
steel 57, 58–9, 61, 82
strontium (Sr) 9, 71
sulfur (S) 25, 46–7, 77

tellurium (Te) 23, 82
tennessine (Ts) 124, 125
thorium (Th) 110, 111
thulium (Tm) 93, 94
tin (Sn) 62, 80–1, 106
titanium (Ti) 54, 97
transuraniums 120–5

uranium (U) 25, 28, 73, 109–14

valency 17

water 8, 10–11, 21, 37

X-rays 31, 87, 93, 105, 116
xenon (Xe) 84–5

ytterbium (Yb) 93, 94, 95
yttrium (Y) 72, 88, 92, 93

zinc (Zn) 30, 63, 64–5, 78, 79
zirconium (Zr) 72, 120